War in Korea

THE REPORT OF A WOMAN COMBAT CORRESPONDENT

photographs by Carl Mydans and others

DOUBLEDAY & COMPANY, INC.

Garden City, New York

DEDICATION

*This book is for the men of the United Nations
who lie together in final fraternity
in the unmarked graves of Korea.*

FOREWORD

This book tries to report the main phases of the Korean war as I saw it. With the exception of four weeks in November, I was almost continuously at the war fronts from June through December. I have selected the episodes and anecdotes that I thought pictured the war most realistically. I have tried to show how the enemy struck, how we fought back, and what we have learned about our weaknesses, our strength, and our future.

MARGUERITE HIGGINS

Seoul, Jan. 1, 1951

CONTENTS

ILLUSTRATIONS

CHAPTER **1**

JOURNEY INTO WAR

The Red invasion of South Korea on Sunday, June 25, 1950, exploded in Tokyo like a delayed-action bomb. The first reports of the dawn attack were nonchalantly received by the duty officer at the Dai Ichi building. He didn't even bother to wake General MacArthur and tell him. But within a few hours the swift advance warned us of the power of the attackers. South Korea, the last non-Communist outpost in North Asia, was crumbling. America had to decide at once whether to lend fighting support to its South Korean protégé or cede it outright to the Reds.

This decision was still hanging fire two days later when my plane roared toward the heart of the Korean war zone under a flashing jet-fighter cover. The plane was headed for the besieged South Korean capital of Seoul to bring out the last of the embattled American civilians. Four newspaper correspondents were the only passengers: Keyes Beech of the Chicago *Daily News*, Frank Gibney of *Time*, Burton Crane of the New York *Times*, and myself.

We were to become the only eyewitnesses to America's entry into the battle for Korea. America began this battle unprepared. And today many hastily dug graves bear witness to the shocking price of underestimating the enemy.

But despite the many tragedies of Korea, we know now that it is fortunate for our world that it resisted Red aggression at that time and in that place. Korea has served as a kind of international alarm clock to wake up the world.

There is a dangerous gap between the mobilized might of the free world and the armaments of the Red world— the Red world which, since 1945, has been talking peace and rushing preparations for war. Korea ripped away our complacency, our smug feeling that all we had to do for our safety was to build bigger atomic bombs. Korea has shown how weak America was. It has shown how desperately we needed to arm and to produce tough, hard-fighting foot soldiers. It was better to find this out in Korea and in June of 1950 than on our own shores and possibly too late.

Nothing can make up for the licking we took in the Korean prelude to the Third World War. But those men in their icy graves will have died for something vital if their warning galvanizes us to the point of becoming so strong that we will win, at the least possible cost, the struggle we cannot escape because the enemy will not cease attacking.

It is just barely possible that if we confront the enemy with obviously superior armed strength at every important testing point in the world, he will back down without a fight. But I doubt it. There may be strategic halts in the Communist-armed expansion, halts of several years. They will be merely periods of regroupment. The Third World War is on. It began in Korea, and I'm glad the first battles I covered were so far away from San Francisco and New York.

But as we four correspondents flew toward Seoul it was only the beginning of the story. The dangers of that first plane ride to Seoul did not greatly concern us, because we were all so relieved to be on the job at last. In the first forty-eight hours after the Korean story broke, it looked as if fate, public relations, officers, and Red Yaks were all conspiring to keep us from flying to Korea to cover the biggest story in the world. At one time during those hectic hours we were actually halfway to Kimpo airfield near Seoul, aboard a big four-motored C-54. But news of a Yak strafing of the field turned the plane back. In desperation we flew to southern Japan, determined to get to Korea by fishing boat if necessary. Fortunately we didn't have to resort to that—through a lucky fluke we had been able to hitch this ride in the evacuation plane.

At the last moment Gibney had tried to dissuade me from going along, insisting that Korea was no place for a woman. But, for me, getting to Korea was more than just a story. It was a personal crusade. I felt that my position as a correspondent was at stake. Here I represented one of

the world's most noted newspapers as its correspondent
in that area. I could not let the fact that I was a woman
jeopardize my newspaper's coverage of the war. Failure to
reach the front would undermine all my arguments that I
was entitled to the same assignment breaks as any man. It
would prove that a woman as a correspondent was a handicap to the New York *Herald Tribune.*

The pilot of our plane, a young veteran of World War
II, told us that his instructions, on arriving in Kimpo, were
to swoop low over the field and try to sight Americans.
"If we don't see any," he said, "it means we get the hell out
but fast—the field is in enemy hands. A green flare means
we land."

About an hour later we were circling over the rubble-
strewn field with its white, shell-pocked administration
building. At the end of the strip we spotted two planes in
flames. Apparently they had been strafed only a matter of
minutes before we appeared. Then, almost simultaneously, all of us saw a group of some thirty Americans.
They signaled us with all the intensity of the shipwrecked
who fear the rescue ship will pass them by.

After we landed we got the big news from Lieutenant
Colonel Peter Scott, who was busily burning documents
on the field. Seoul was still in friendly hands—the correspondents who had fled the city that morning had been
premature. In fact, the sixty officers of the Korean Military
Advisory Group (KMAG) had moved back into the city
that afternoon on direct orders from General MacArthur.
MacArthur had been given responsibility for American

personnel in Korea at the eleventh hour, after the outbreak of actual hostilities.

We had a world scoop. Keyes, speaking for all four of us, told the pilot that we were going to stay and go into the city with the colonel. The pilot shook his head as if he thought we were sadly crazy, but we had no more interest in that particular plane.

There was plenty of transportation handy. The panicky Americans had abandoned scores of nice new Buicks, Dodges, and jeeps. Some had been carefully locked, out of habit, but most of the owners had realized the futility of the gesture and left their keys behind. Just about dusk we set out through the rain, in convoy. Machine guns sputtered in the distance.

"They are at least seven miles away," Colonel Scott said, "but there's no point in hanging around. The road into town can easily be cut by guerillas."

The road to Seoul was crowded with refugees. There were hundreds of Korean women with babies bound papoose-style to their backs and huge bundles on their heads. There were scores of trucks, elaborately camouflaged with branches. South Korean soldiers in jeeps and on horses were streaming in both directions.

It was a moving and rather terrifying experience, there on that rainy road to Seoul, to have the crowds cheer and wave as our little caravan of Americans went by. Their obvious confidence in anything American had a pathetic quality. I thought then, as I was to think often in later days, "I hope we don't let them down."

In Seoul we drew up before the bleak, sprawling, graystone building which housed the Korean Military Advisory Group headquarters. There we found Colonel Sterling Wright, the acting head of the advisory group. He met us with the news that the situation was "fluid but hopeful." Maps and files were even then being moved back into the rickety building. Because of the confused South Korean reports, Wright's staff of military advisers had, that very afternoon, started out of the city. Since he had no idea that help was coming from anywhere, it had seemed to Colonel Wright that the jig was up and the battle for Korea all over except for the mopping up.

But halfway down the road to Suwon reports reached him that the picture painted by the Koreans was far too black. Then a message from General MacArthur arrived and turned the group right around. I saw the message there in the basket on Wright's desk. It announced the arrival of an American survey team, charged with finding out what was needed to save Korea. In typical MacArthur style it exhorted: "Be of good cheer. Momentous events are pending." It was the first hint that American arms might be thrown into the Korean fight.

Actually, almost at this very moment, President Truman was announcing the big decision to commit American air and naval power in the attempt to prevent Communist seizure of all Korea.

I remember vividly the midnight briefing during that first siege of Seoul. "The South Koreans have a pathological fear of tanks," Wright told us. "That is part of the reason for all this retreating. They could handle them if they would only use the weapons we have given them properly." I often thought later, when Colonel Wright saw what those same tanks did to American troops, how much he must have regretted his words. But he was certainly not alone in his belief. It was just another example of how much we underestimated both the enemy and his equipment.

According to Wright, the Communists had had the advantage of complete surprise in their attack. The head of KMAG, Brigadier General William Roberts, was en route to the United States for a new assignment. Colonel Wright himself was not even in Korea, but vacationing in Japan. Of course it was well known that the North Korean Communists had ordered civilians to evacuate a two-mile stretch bordering the 38th parallel. They had also been showering leaflets daily, threatening invasion, and had even lobbed some mortars into the mountain border city of Kaesong. But nobody took it seriously. Their excuse was that the enemy had been making threats for six months and nothing had happened.

Unfortunately, free countries have a chronic disposition to ignore the threats made by dictatorships. Hitler told us what he was going to do. The North Koreans told us what they were going to do, and so did the Chinese. But because we didn't like what they told us, we didn't believe them.

In the first few hours of the attack the South Korean Army fought well, retreating to prepared positions. It soon became clear that the main Communist thrust was in the Uijongbu corridor just north of Seoul. The menacing Soviet tanks headed the onslaught. At first the South Koreans bravely tackled the tanks with highly inadequate 2.36 bazookas. They saw their volleys bounce off the monsters, and many squads armed with grenades and Molotov cocktails went to suicidal deaths in frenzied efforts to stop the advance. The decisive crack-up came when one of the South Korean divisions failed to follow through on schedule with a counterattack in the Seoul corridor.

But this night the South Korean retreat had been temporarily halted just north of Seoul, where the troops had rallied. As we left headquarters General Chee, then South Korean Chief of Staff, bustled past us toward his offices. He was resplendent in his brightly polished American helmet and American uniform, and told us, "We fightin' hard now. Things gettin' better."

I had been assigned to Colonel Wright's headquarters billets; the other three newsmen were housed with one of his deputies. And, in spite of General Chee's good cheer, I followed some inner warning and lay down fully clothed. It seemed as if I had hardly closed my eyes when Colonel Wright's aide burst in. "Get up!" he shouted. "They've broken through—we have to run for it."

CHAPTER 2

THE FIRST RETREAT

Soon after the lieutenant announced the Communist break-through, mortars started bursting around our billet. Piling into separate jeeps, the colonel and his executive officer in one, the aide and I in the other, we rushed toward the big bridge across the Han River—the only escape route. As we raced through the rainy darkness a sheet of orange flame tore the sky.

"Good God, there goes the bridge," said the lieutenant.

We were trapped. The Han River lay between us and safety to the south, and the only bridge had been dynamited. We turned our jeep back to the Korean Military Advisory Group headquarters. There in the darkness, punctuated by shellbursts, the fifty-nine men of Colonel Wright's staff were slowly gathering.

Colonel Wright told us, with disgust in his voice, "The

South Koreans blew up that bridge without even bothering to give us warning, and they blew it much too soon. Most of the town is still in their hands. They blew that bridge with truckloads of their own troops on the main span. They've killed hundreds of their own men."

Our situation was certainly both serious and highly confusing. We had no idea why the South Korean commanders had suddenly bolted. We couldn't tell from the sporadic gunfire around us where the enemy was or how big a break-through had been made.

A number of officers began spreading the idea that if we didn't get out fast we would be captured. The murmurings grew to a nervous crescendo. For a while I was afraid that we might have the unpleasant development of panic in our own American ranks. But Colonel Wright, with quiet authority, easily got things in hand.

"Now listen, everybody," he said. "Nobody is going to go high-tailing off by himself. We're all in this together. We're going to take it easy until we're sure we've collected everybody. Then we're going to try to find an alternate route out of the city—a rail bridge, perhaps—so that we can save our vehicles."

We certainly tried. We assembled a convoy of sixty jeeps, trucks, and weapons carriers and started off with headlights ablaze. Although we knew that we might run into the enemy at any moment, we drove for several hours looking in vain for a rail span that could support our convoy. As we toured the town I kept asking KMAG officials if they had seen the other three correspondents.

Finally Major Sedberry, the operations officer, told me, "Oh, they got out in plenty of time. The three of them came by the office and I told them to head fast across the bridge for Suwon. They're probably there right now scooping you."

My concern immediately turned into a very different sort. Deep inside I had complete confidence that somehow we would get over that river, even if we had to swim. But I had no confidence whatever that I would get out in time to compete with my rivals, whom I grumpily pictured safe and smug in Suwon.

During one long wait, while a scouting party was looking for a place to ferry across the river, Colonel Wright noticed my gloomy air. "What's the matter, kid," he asked, "afraid you won't get your story out?" And after a pause he offered, "Look, stick by this radio truck and we'll try to send out a message for you if you keep it short."

It was now growing light, and in my elation I immediately got out my typewriter, put it on the front of the jeep, and typed furiously. Streams of retreating South Korean soldiers were then passing our stationary convoy. Many of them turned their heads and gaped at the sight of an American woman, dressed in a navy-blue skirt, flowered blouse, and bright blue sweater, typing away on a jeep in the haze of daybreak. I got my copy in all right. But as far as I know, communications never were established long enough to send it.

As I was typing the last part of my story, artillery began

zeroing in. It was obvious now that if we didn't want to be captured we would have to abandon our equipment and wade or ferry across the river. When we reached the riverbank we found masses of refugees and South Korean soldiers in a panicky press. Some of the soldiers were firing at boatmen and raftsmen in an attempt to force them to come to our side of the river. Other soldiers were defeating their own aims by rushing aboard any available craft in such numbers that they swamped the tiny boats. It was only by holding back the rush at rifle point that we got our band across the river. We were harassed all the while by steady but inaccurate rifle fire.

Once across the river, there was nothing to do but walk across the mountain trail toward Suwon. Our single file of soldiers was soon joined by a huge stream of refugees. Even the Korean Minister of the Interior, who was once a Buddhist priest, trudged along with a pack on his back. South Korean soldiers in GI uniforms also fell in line. Before long the Americans were leading a ragamuffin army of tattered soldiers, old men, diplomats, children, and a woman war correspondent.

I was very conscious of being the only woman in the group. I was determined not to give trouble in any way, shape, or form. Luckily, I am a good walker, and by enormous good fortune I was wearing flat-heeled shoes. For much of the march I was close to the head of the column.

After we had sloughed southward over the muddy path for about an hour I heard a steady drone in the sky and looked up, startled. Then the silvery fighters came nearer and started looping and diving over Seoul. My heart pounded with excitement—this must be part of the "momentous event" mentioned in MacArthur's message. For they were American planes. The realization that American air power was in the war hit everybody at the same time. The Koreans around me screamed and yelled with joy. Women from an adjacent village rushed out to grab my hand and point to the sky in ecstasy.

It was a sweet moment, but the savoring was brief. The march was far too grim and sad to permit lengthy rejoicing. It was plain that in this sector the Koreans were in complete rout. We saw many throw down their weapons and turn and run simply at the sight of our American group going southward.

After we had hiked for about four hours, a jeep showed up on the dirt trail. It already contained five Korean soldiers, but somehow a KMAG colonel, a Korean officer, Colonel Lee, and I all squeezed in. Our mission was to go ahead to Suwon and send back transportation to the now very weary group.

The KMAG officer and Colonel Lee became increasingly distressed by the disorderly retreat around us. Finally, at the main road, they got out to try to round up stragglers so they could be reorganized. I was now alone in the jeep with six Koreans who could not speak a word of English.

When we reached Suwon, I had two messages to deliver, in addition to the request for transportation. One was the information that Seoul had fallen. The other was a request from KMAG for a "general bombing north of the Han River line." I was to get these messages to Ambassador John J. Muccio and Major General John Church. General Church had, overnight, become head of the American Advance Command.

Suwon, the new temporary capital, was in an extremely confused state. It took me several hours to find General Church and Ambassador Muccio and give them the messages. A few minutes after I had finished my job Ambassador Muccio called the handful of correspondents together (a total of five) and asked us to go away. He said we were a nuisance.

At this gathering I learned that my three newspaper colleagues had not only never gotten across the bridge but that it had exploded right under them, wounding Crane and Gibney. They were wandering around the Agricultural Building with bloodstained undershirts tied around their foreheads. So twelve hours after the first fall of Seoul, and several hours after American air power entered the war, the only four reporters with eyewitness accounts were still in Korea and the story was untold.

Burton, Keyes, and I decided to fly back to Itazuke in Japan, where we could file our reports. When we got there we heard some news that made us fully appreciate our good luck in getting out of Seoul when we did. The French news-agency correspondent, as well as most of the staff of the French and British embassies, had been captured at just about the time we were crossing the river.

Back in Korea the next day, General Douglas Mac-
Arthur's famous plane, the *Bataan,* was sitting on the airstrip. We learned that the Supreme Commander had gone
by jeep to the Han River to see for himself what was
needed. I was crouched by the side of the windy airstrip
typing a quick story on his visit when the general himself
appeared. He was clad in his famous Bataan gold-braid
hat and summer khakis with the shirt open at the collar.
He smoked a corncob pipe. He was accompanied by a
whole retinue of assorted generals, most of whom I'd
never seen before.

On seeing me on the airstrip, the general came over to
say hello and then asked if I would like a lift back to
Tokyo. Since the *Bataan* offered the only means of flying
back to communications and getting the story out, I
gladly accepted.

My presence on the plane, I later learned, considerably
miffed the four bureau chiefs: Russ Brines of the Associated Press, Earnest Hoberecht of the United Press,
Howard Handleman of International News Service, and
Roy McCartney of Reuters. Until then they had thought
they had the story of MacArthur's trip completely to
themselves. We later dubbed these four correspondents
"the palace guard" because they were the only ones privi-
ledged to accompany MacArthur on his front-line visits.
On this plane trip, to the further annoyance of the palace
guard, Major General Whitney told me that the general
had given the other correspondents a briefing in the
morning, adding, "I'm sure he would like to talk to you

now. Why don't you go up to his cabin and see him?" Of course I did.

In personal conversation General MacArthur is a man of graciousness and great lucidity. So far as I am concerned, he is without the poseur traits of which I have heard him accused. It has always seemed to me most unfortunate that the general held himself so aloof from most of the newspapermen in Tokyo. I am convinced that if he would spare the time, even once a month, to see correspondents, he would dissolve most of the hostility felt toward his command and toward him personally. The lack of contact between MacArthur, who shapes many Far Eastern events, and the newspapermen, who must write of these events, has made it very difficult for correspondents, no matter how talented or well-meaning. There has been some bad reporting by those who had to rely on guesswork. This, in turn, has increased the aloofness on the part of MacArthur and his command.

It is said that MacArthur's lofty isolation from all except a few very close, loyal advisers has won the respect of the Japanese and so furthered the aims of the occupation. Certainly the unquestioning, almost mystic devotion rendered him by those close to him forms part of his legend. But I think that it might be better for the American people if the store of wisdom he possesses were shared with them through greater accessibility.

Washington had sent MacArthur to Korea with orders to find out whether air and naval power alone could save the South Korean republic. Reversing the earlier decision

MYDANS

A sergeant after the battle.

MYDANS

General Douglas MacArthur with President Syngman Rhee.

MYDANS

Miss Higgins after landing at Suwon.

MYDANS

Major General William F. Dean as he led the United Nations Forces during the early stages of the war.

The late Lieutenant General Walton H. Walker, former Eighth Army Commander.

to write off Korea, President Truman was apparently now determined to save this anti-Communist bastion if possible.

General MacArthur had come away from his front-line view of the South Korean retreat with the conviction that if America wanted to save Korea, ground troops would have to be committed. "It is certain that the South Koreans badly need an injection of ordered American strength," he told me. "The South Korean soldiers are in good physical condition and could be rallied with example and leadership. Give me two American divisions and I can hold Korea."

General MacArthur's belief that two divisions could "hold Korea" was based on recommendations from KMAG and his forward commanders. It showed how disastrously they still underestimated the enemy. As I look back, it seems to me that we all underestimated, not so much the North Koreans themselves, but the extent to which they were equipped and backed by the Soviet Union.

In the light of the previous attitude of the Joint Chiefs of Staff, MacArthur was considerably surprised by President Truman's decision to go to South Korea's aid, but he agreed with the change in policy. Although created under United Nations auspices, Korea was actually a protégé of the United States. We had strongly encouraged South Korea to defy Soviet communism. The American Congress had even legislated that aid to Korea would be immediately cut off if a single Communist was discovered in the National Assembly.

Now we had a job to do. On the plane that night General MacArthur said, "The moment I reach Tokyo, I shall send President Truman my recommendation for the immediate dispatch of American divisions to Korea. But I have no idea whether he will accept my recommendation."

CHAPTER **3**

PANIC

On June thirtieth I started back to Suwon, and for the last time, although I didn't know that then. It seemed incredible that only three days ago we had landed at Seoul, now one retreat away.

Emergency had telescoped so many events that it was impossible to grasp the full meaning of what was happening. I simply had an urgent impulse to get back to the scene of action as fast as I could, before too many things had rushed past me.

As our heavy, unarmed ammunition ship rumbled off the runway the crew was in a fine state of nerves. For the past two days Yak fighters had been spurting bullets at the Suwon strip. The day before a transport had been shot down going into the same field.

" 'Firecracker' is the code to call for help if a Yak jumps

you," we had been told by the operations briefing officers. "There'll be an umbrella of jets and Mustangs over
you as you start across the mountains."

Our pilot was Lieutenant Donald Marsh. He was a
veteran of the fighting for Guam and knew what we might
run into. As we approached the deep, rocky inlets of brilliant blue water that are Pusan Bay, Marsh warned us,
"In a few minutes we reach hot weather. Put on your
chutes and grab a helmet." And then, after glancing over
his shoulder in the direction of the big 155-millimeter
shells we were carrying, he added flatly, "Though I don't
know what in Christ good a chute will do if we do get
hit."

I felt the rush of fear that was to become so familiar
in the next weeks. It seemed to turn into a trapped ball
of breath that was pressing against my heart. I could see
by the faces of the crew that I was definitely not worrying alone. The radio operator took his place beneath the
glass-dome turret of the C-54. In a few moments somebody saw an unidentified plane, but it didn't see us. And
that was all.

But the ominous atmosphere continued even after
we had bumped and scraped to a stop on the Suwon airfield. We had had to brake hard to avoid the wrecked,
bullet-splattered planes at the end of the runway.

As I climbed out of the plane, fervently promising myself never to ride on another ammunition ship, I was
greeted by a dour army colonel. He was the nervous, of-

ficious type that the Army seems to have a talent for producing.

"You'll have to go back, young lady," the colonel said. "You can't stay here. There may be trouble."

Somewhat wearily, I brought out my stock answer to this solicitude. "I wouldn't be here if there were no trouble. Trouble is news, and the gathering of news is my job."

The colonel's too familiar attitude was discouraging. I had hoped that my performance under fire in the exit from Seoul would have ended further arguments that "the front is no place for a woman." But it was to be many weeks before I was accepted on an equal basis with the men. Interestingly enough, most of my difficulties were with headquarters officials, especially those who themselves had never been directly on a firing line. I never had any trouble when I got to the front lines.

As I was answering the colonel I saw a jeep approaching, and to my delight the driver was Lieutenant May—Colonel Sterling Wright's aide and a comrade of our long march across the mountains out of Seoul. I knew he was on my side.

"Hey, Lieutenant," I shouted, "how about a ride back to headquarters?" Lieutenant May nodded, and as the jeep swept by I jumped aboard and we were off before the colonel could do anything but sputter.

Even in twenty-four hours one temporary American headquarters at Suwon had changed, and, from a newsman's point of view, for the worse. Reinforcements of

Tokyo colonels and majors were bustling about, holding tight to information they imagined was secret. This Tokyo contingent was rapidly taking over the job from the veterans of the Korean Military Advisory Group, our friends of the retreat from Seoul. The latter, led by Colonel Wright, had dealt with us as friends, caught in a situation equally difficult for all. Now the American journalists were being treated more like Communist agents than as fellow citizens.

The moment the jeep rattled into the pine-dotted Suwon headquarters I sensed another crisis. It was 6 P.M. In the main wooden building little knots of officers were talking in low voices. Major Greenwood of KMAG spotted me as I got out of the jeep, walked over with elaborate casualness, and said, "Don't go far away from headquarters. It looks bad again."

Looking back later, I was shocked to remember that Walt Greenwood was the only officer there who bothered to warn the correspondents and enlisted men of their possible danger. The events of that evening provided the most appalling example of panic that I have ever seen.

By the time I arrived at headquarters, Tom Lambert of the Associated Press and Keyes Beech—by now an experienced man at retreats—already had their wind up. The rest of the correspondents were busy housekeeping. They had taken over the only unoccupied shack, and photographers and newsmen were busy sweeping out the filth and collecting straw on which to lay blankets. But Keyes, Tom, and I all felt too worried to be domestic. We strolled up

to the main building where low-toned conferences were
still going on among the officers.

"We've got the jeep all set in case there's trouble,"
Keyes told me. "And there's a place in it for you."

"Thanks a lot, Keyes," I answered with real gratitude.
I hoped that the invitation meant I was winning an ally
from the male correspondents' camp.

Strategically located near the conference room, we
tried to get information from the officers, Korean and
American, who were streaming in and out. We heard
something vague about a convoy of fifty North Korean
trucks and tanks that had somehow forded the Han River
and were in our vicinity. But no one would tell us anything definite.

The general in charge of the Tokyo contingent, which
was then called the Korean Survey Group and later became the American Advance Command in Korea, was
seven miles down the road at the repeater station. This
station afforded the only means of direct telephonic com-
munication with Tokyo.

It turned out that during the critical conference, all that
the group had to rely on were reports from Korean intelligence. And these reports were as unreliable at that stage
as the South Korean Army itself.

Suddenly the doors of the conference room scraped
open. We heard the thump of running feet and a piercing
voice, addressed to the officers within the room: "Head for
the airfield."

We three correspondents looked at each other. Who

was heading for the airfield and why? The uncertainty was frightening, maddening. Almost simultaneously we jumped up and raced into the building. Our questions were met with a flat, "You're not allowed in here." Down the hall we met an elderly colonel rushing wildly toward the door.

He had to slow down because I was practically blocking his way. "Why," I asked him quickly, "if there is something wrong, don't we all take the road south to Taejon?" (Taejon is about eighty road miles south of Suwon.)

Flinging his arms high in the air in an operatic gesture, the colonel answered, "We're surrounded, we're surrounded," and pushed past.

Keyes and I glanced at each other quickly. If this were true, the beautiful independence of having our own jeep ready didn't mean a thing. Our only chance of survival was to stick by the guys with the guns and communications with Tokyo and the United States Air Force.

The panic of the next few minutes jumbled events and emotions so wildly that I can remember only episodic flashes. I remember a furious sergeant stalking out of the Signal Corps room and saying to Keyes, "Those sons of bitches are trying to save their own hides—there are planes coming, but the brass won't talk. They're afraid there won't be room for everybody."

The rumor that the officers were trying to escape without the rest swirled around the camp like a dust storm. From then on every mess sergeant, jeep driver, code clerk, and correspondent had just one idea—to get hold of every and any vehicle around. Any South Korean who owned four wheels and who was unlucky enough to be near that headquarters that night was on foot from that second forward. That was the fastest convoy ever formed, and probably the most disheveled.

Someone shouted, "The Reds are down the road." Someone else bellowed, "No, they're at the airfield." Then Major Greenwood came to us with the news, "We're going to defend the airstrip. Better be ready."

I watched Tom and Keyes grimly arming themselves with carbines, checking their clips. "My God," Keyes said, almost to himself, "do they really think this handful of men can hold that airstrip? They're out of their minds." There were about sixty men and myself. That was one time when I wished that my rifle experience extended beyond one afternoon on the range.

So much had happened it seemed impossible that barely five or six minutes had elapsed since the wild breakup of the conference. Keyes, Tom, and Gordon Walker of the *Christian Science Monitor*, with carbines in hand, were jammed into the jeep with me. We had a young sergeant riding shotgun.

All I had with me was my typewriter and a toothbrush. In the first retreat in Seoul, where I had had to abandon all my personal things, I'd learned that they were all I really needed.

The first jeeps started bouncing toward the airfield without orders or direction. They were filled with infuriated GIs determined not to be left behind by the brass.

Correspondents and photographers, hitching rides as best they could, joined the race.

At the field Major Greenwood did his best to organize a perimeter defense of the bomb-pocked strip. Mines were laid, machine guns entrenched, small-arms ammunition distributed. It began to look to me like a fair start toward a Korean Corregidor.

Much later I learned more about this projected last-ditch stand at the field. Some planes really were due that evening from Japan, not enough to take everybody, but at least a start in the evacuation. Our small force was supposed to hold the field until the planes arrived. Actually they never arrived at all.

Suddenly plans changed. Rumors started spreading that the brass had decided to take the escape road directly south to Taejon.

"So we are not surrounded after all," I said to Keyes. "This is a fine way to find out."

Distrusting all the rumor and counterrumor, our jeep-load of correspondents decided that we would stay put until the very last minute, to try to judge for ourselves what the situation was. We had heard that Colonel Wright had gone back to the suddenly abandoned headquarters to try to get word to his advisory officers with the South Korean troops. He was going to instruct them to leave their charges and head for Taejon, but it appeared certain that there would not be enough time to permit his officers to catch up with our convoy.

This was the second time in a week that American of-

ficers had been ordered to leave the front. Their departure, of course, didn't help the precarious morale of the
South Korean Army.

About 11 P.M. we decided to follow the crowd of Americans unhappily bumping southward on the rutted dirt
road. Then the torrential Korean rains started. Korean
nights are cool even in summer, and with this pitiless
downpour the temperature was like a foggy winter's day
in San Francisco. None of the men were wearing more
than shirts and slacks, and I was still in my blouse and
skirt. There had been no time to buy or scrounge a khaki
shirt and pants.

The rain pounded down without letup during the entire
seven miserable hours in our completely open jeep. The
blankets we put over us soon were soaked through, and
we just sat helplessly, as drenched as if we had gone
swimming with our clothes on.

The road turned to slithery mud and the rivers became
enormously swollen. At one point Keyes, who did much of
the driving, swore that we must be lost because the
bridge we were crossing appeared to be a long pier leading into the ocean. We all got out and groped around
ahead of the jeep, and finally convinced him that it was
merely a terribly wide river.

I was sitting scrunched in the front seat between Keyes
and Walker, straining to see the road, when suddenly the
jeep skidded viciously in the mud.

"Hold on, this is it!" shouted Keyes. He fought the
wheel desperately as we teetered on the edge of a steep

drop on our right. Finally the jeep swerved and the front wheels crashed into the ditch on our left. It wasn't as bad as the one we had missed but it was deep enough. All five of us, struggling in the mud and rain, couldn't get the jeep back onto the road. Feeling guilty at my inadequate strength, I started out to look for a Korean farmhouse where we might get help. It was about 5 A.M. and a dim gray dawn was breaking. Through the downpour I sighted a Korean thatched hut across the brilliant green rice paddy. It was, for Korea, a well-to-do farm. The Koreans were stretched out on the wooden floor of their porch. When I woke up the family of several men, a woman, and two children, they accepted the situation with true oriental calm. They showed no surprise whatever at seeing a rain-drenched white woman standing there in the dawn, and two of the men promptly followed me back to the jeep. Their muscle provided enough extra power to wrench it back onto the road.

I had been worrying because we had absolutely nothing to give the Koreans as recompense, but apparently they expected nothing. The two white-clad men walked away even as we started consulting among ourselves as to what we could do for them.`

That miserable drive ended about an hour later. We rolled into Taejon about 6 A.M. and headed for the main government building, a sturdy, rambling, two-story brick structure. It looked deserted, but we went up the stairs into the main conference room. There we were surprised to find General Church sitting all by himself at a long, felt-covered conference table. A spare, small-boned man, the general looked very alone.

As it turned out, there had been no reason to hurry. The panic was all for nothing. There were no Communist troops within miles of Suwon. In fact, it was more than three days before it fell, and groups of American correspondents and officers re-entered the city a number of times before its final seizure.

It seemed that General Church had preceded us by only a few hours. But he had had time to communicate with Tokyo. He looked somewhat quizzically at these four miserable, rain-soaked creatures. I was shaking like a wet puppy, quite unable to control the chattering of my teeth, my gabardine skirt dripping little pools of rain water on the rug.

The general said quietly, "You may be interested to know that two companies of American troops were airlifted into southern Korea this morning."

"Well, here we go—America's at war," I thought to myself, and hardly wondered at my own matter-of-factness. (We were so completely cut off from the outside world that we had no way of knowing then, or for several days, that this was a United Nations action.) By now my state of utter physical discomfort, the cold, and the cruel need for sleep left no room for any emotion.

Thinking of our retreat and reports of new rout all along the front, I asked the general, "Don't you think it's too late?"

"Certainly not," he said confidently. "It will be differ-

ent when the Americans get here. We'll have people we
can rely on. To tell you the truth, we've been having a
pretty rough time with the South Koreans. We can't put
backbone into them. What are you going to do with
troops that won't stay where they're put? We have no
way of knowing whether the South Korean reports are
accurate or just wild rumor. It will be better when we
have our own organization. It may take one or two divisions." (General Church later changed his opinion of the
caliber of South Korean soldiers and was one of the first
to include large numbers in his own 24th Infantry Division.)

The general added that the first Americans would be
deployed directly north of Taejon to safeguard key
bridges between this city and Suwon. Troops would arrive in Taejon, he said, in a matter of hours.

None of us, military or civilian, had the remotest idea
of what we were really up against: a total of thirteen to
fifteen enemy divisions. This meant approximately one
hundred and fifty thousand well-armed, hard-fighting
Reds, equipped with the only heavy tanks in that part
of the world. Actually, Major General Charles A. Wil-
loughby, MacArthur's Director of Intelligence in Tokyo,
had reported to Washington that the enemy was massing
this war potential. But certainly none of the soldiers in
the field seemed to know that his report realistically measured enemy strength.

I asked the general, "How long will it be before we
can mount an offensive?"

"Oh, two weeks or so—maybe a month," he replied.

"But suppose the Russkis intervene?" asked Keyes.

"If they intervene, we'll hurl them back too."

And that ended the interview. We walked back into the rain with two tremendous stories: the flight from Suwon and the arrival of the American soldiers. And here we were again with the same old communications problem. How were we to get our stories out?

Tom Lambert, who was with the Associated Press, had a twenty-four-hour-a-day deadline. He suddenly remembered a rumor that Ambassador John J. Muccio had a line to Tokyo at his quarters in Taejon. Remembering his hostility to the press a few days earlier, we hated to ask for anything. But we were desperate.

When the ambassador opened the door of his small gray house in the American-built compound in Taejon's suburb, his face clouded. Beyond him we could see an open, blazing fire—the most beautiful sight I've ever seen in my life—an open whisky bottle perched on the mantel, and a melee of tired, distraught Americans in the process of thawing out. Our faces spoke frank longing to be invited in, and the ambassador must have been feeling compassionate, for he let us in. Never has the warmth of a fire or the burning glow of a straight shot of whisky felt so magnificent.

But there was no phone. The ambassador did tell us, however, that some correspondents had been using a phone down at the United States Information Service. Tom and I, because we were the two on immediate deadline, promptly rushed out the door and hitched ourselves a ride. (We had left our own jeep at headquarters.)

The phone was there all right, in the rickety first-floor room just across from the Taejon rail station. Tom, by a fluke, got through to his office in about twenty minutes—often it took two or three hours. Although we were tremendously relieved to have communications at last, we were both disappointed that we had no time to write out our stories. We simply couldn't risk losing this opportunity and so had to dictate our pieces straight off. This was particularly difficult for me, since I was used to daily newspaper techniques rather than news-agency techniques. I had never before been faced with the necessity of organizing a story in my head for immediate dictation.

This was to prove the least of my troubles. I was a one-man bureau, and so had no one in Tokyo to whom I could give my story. Tom asked the Associated Press if they would help me. The Associated Press is, of course, a co-operative enterprise in which the New York *Herald Tribune* is an owner paper. They would ordinarily try to help out a correspondent of a member newspaper.

But after I had dictated only about three paragraphs, Mrs. Barbara Brines, wife of the Tokyo bureau manager, cut in excitedly with, "That's all we can take, Marguerite, that's all we can take."

I was, of course, frantic. Was that long, horrible ride, the cold, the fear, all of it, to be for nothing? There was only one thing to do. I would try to get Tokyo back, call the Press Club, and try to find one of my colleagues who could help me out. I thought immediately of Joe Fromm of the *U. S. News & World Report,* one of the ablest and hardest-working members of the Tokyo Press Club. Joe agreed at once to take the story. But by this time the USIS room had filled with correspondents pressing hard for the use of the phone.

Under these psychological pressures I slashed the Suwon episode to about two paragraphs and compressed the rest of the really important events into five or six paragraphs. I felt miserable and frustrated.

The battle of communications which began there at Taejon continued throughout the war. The Army, it seemed to me, consistently managed to make a very difficult situation frightful. At Taejon, for instance, the USIS phone was taken away from us by the end of the next day. Time after time correspondents, who were working in a state of utter exhaustion, found themselves forced into the attitude of "to hell with the quality—the miracle is to get the story out at all."

I know that never once during the Korean war have I been satisfied with the writing and organization of a single story. I know all of us in the beginning kept thinking, "Well, next time maybe there will be more of a chance to think it through," or, "Next time I won't be so tired." But in those early days it was commonplace for Keyes, Tom, and myself to find each other slumped over our typewriters, collapsed in sleep in the middle of a story.

The coverage of the Korean campaign has been dominated by this situation. Getting the story has been about one fifth of the problem; the principle energies of the reporters had to be devoted to finding some means of transmission.

After dictating my story that morning, I rushed back into the drizzle to try to hitch a ride for Tom and myself. Keyes and Gordon were waiting for us at the ambassador's. I flagged a Korean officer who turned out to be an exceptionally neat, well-dressed fellow who spoke English quite well. Tom climbed in back with the officer, and I sat in front with the driver. Feeling comparatively chipper with the relief of sending his story, Tom clapped the Korean officer heartily on the shoulder.

"Hey, Buster," said Tom, "do you fight in this man's army?"

"Well," answered the officer politely, "I plan to. I have just returned from Fort Benning."

"That's fine, Buster," said Tom jovially, clapping him on the shoulder again. "And what do you do?"

"I shall reorganize the South Koreans' defenses," the officer replied. "You see, I have just been appointed the new Chief of the Korean Army. My name is Major General Kim Il Kuan."

CHAPTER 4

THE FIRST SKIRMISH

The Korean monsoon was still in full downpour two days later when our jeepload of correspondents started to the front to watch Americans dig in—and die—in their first battle.

As we left the little gray house at Taejon's outskirts around three in the morning, our conversation was as somber as the weather. We were going to Pyontek, where only the day before our forces had been badly strafed by our own planes. This was the first of many incidents which showed how much we needed to improve our ground-air co-ordination. I was assigned now to watch the skies and give warning if I saw a plane.

As we neared Pyontek we had to drive around blackened, still-burning ammo trucks. And by the side of the road were the mutilated bodies of scores of hapless refugees who had been caught in the strafing. The smell of death rose from the ditches and the waterlogged rice paddies on either side of the road.

The conversation, in keeping with the glumness of the hour, turned to epitaphs. Roy McCartney of Reuters, a portly, hard-working young Australian, told us of an inscription he had seen on an unknown British soldier's tomb in Burma. He recited it in full for us there in the wet dawn, as we paused for a C-ration breakfast of frankfurters and beans.

"Here dead we lie because we did not choose
To live and shame the land from which we sprung.
Life, to be sure, is nothing much to lose;
But young men think it is, and we were young."

(I found out later that it is a quotation from A. E. Housman.)

Aside from the general melancholy of the morning, I had some purely personal reasons for being unhappy. There has been some publicity about a feud between me and one of my *Herald Tribune* colleagues. It is quite true that the difficulty existed, and I see no point in being coy about it here.

The simple fact was that my colleague didn't want me to stay in Korea at all. I had cabled the office at home that I very much wanted to stay, that I believed there was more than enough news to share and that the war could be covered on a partnership basis. My colleague disagreed with this to the point where he told me flatly that I would be fired if I didn't get back to Tokyo and stay there. He also added the reassuring information that he didn't believe I had a single friend in Tokyo.

This was a distressing puzzle to me at the time, but I later learned that he was probably right. The Tokyo agency bureau chiefs were furious about a story I had allegedly filed on American bombings north of the 38th parallel. The four chiefs had learned of the proposed bombings before the MacArthur visit to the front lines and had agreed among themselves to keep the story a secret until a fixed date. They had received callbacks on some story of mine (callbacks apparently indicating that they had been scooped) and wrongly believed that I had learned about the bombings from MacArthur and filed the story ahead of their schedule. Since I didn't know anything about their schedule, what they were really doing was accusing me of breaking an agreement to which I was never a party. It is true that I knew about the bombing plans, but from quite another source. I honestly couldn't remember ever filing the bombing story at all, and when I checked the *Herald Tribune* files on my return I found no record of it. But that, of course, was much later. And in the meantime I was caught squarely in the middle of a lot of unpleasant confusion.

I was in such a state of physical exhaustion that I was unusually vulnerable emotionally and really felt baffled and upset. But, whatever the attitude in Tokyo, I found some fine moral support in Korea. Carl ("Stumpy") Mydans of *Time* and *Life*, a wonderfully kind human being, had unwittingly become mixed up in my problem because my colleague had warned him that if he took me to the front I would be fired. I talked it all over with Carl, and he helped me make up my mind with this question, "What is more important to you, Maggie, the experience of covering the Korean war or fears of losing your job?" Right then I decided to go back to the front, no matter what came of it.

But there was no denying that I was heavyhearted. I felt that no matter what the cause of my colleague's hostility, it would be harder on me because I was a woman. Since I was the only woman here doing a daily newspaper job, I was bound to be the target for lots of talk, and this mix-up would supply fresh material. I believed that no matter who was right, I would undoubtedly be blamed.

But I was happily wrong. The men correspondents on the scene in Korea could not have been more fair. They did the only sensible thing, which was to refuse to take sides at all. By the end of the summer the entire situation ended up where it belonged, in the joke department.

But at Pyontek that morning there was only gloom in the air and in my mind. We were all cold and tired by the time we found the battalion command post hidden in a tiny thatched hut surrounded by a sea of mud. Colonel Harold ("Red") Ayres, commander of the first battalion of the 34th Infantry Regiment, shared his command post with a filthy assortment of chickens, pigs, and ducks.

We had barely had time to enjoy a cup of hot coffee when Brigadier General George B. Barth strode into the hut. "Enemy tanks are heading south," he said. "Get me some bazooka teams pronto."

Then, apparently aware of our startled reaction, he added, "Those Communist tanks are going to meet Americans for the first time—Colonel Smith's battalion is up forward. We can depend on him to hold on, but if any tanks do get by those batteries they'll head straight for here."

So America's raw young troops, boys who had reached the Korean front only a few hours before, were going into battle. It was a big moment, and we four knew that we had been cut in on a critical slice of history. We were about to see the beginning of what we later named the long retreat.

I was filled with a very uncomfortable mixture of apprehension and excitement as we followed the bazooka teams to the unknown front. Wrapped in rain-soaked blankets, we traveled swiftly behind the small convoy of trucks and command cars carrying the bazooka and rifle teams. Then, on the crest of a hill, the convoy suddenly halted. We could see soldiers jumping out of the trucks and spreading out on a ridge parallel to the road. The road was clogged with South Korean soldiers in what seemed an endless procession southward. (South Koreans, in these early days, simply appropriated the jeeps or command cars assigned to them and took off individually.) One South Korean soldier on horseback, his helmet camouflaged with bits of branches sticking up at absurd angles, came cantering toward us, shouting, "Tanks! Tanks! Tanks! Go back."

"Now wait a minute," said McCartney in his quiet British tone. "Even if tanks do show, no infantry has been sighted. Tanks can't get off the road, and we can. Let's walk on."

A little farther on we found Lieutenant Charles Payne —a dapper, fast-talking young veteran of World War II. He had been examining the marks of huge tank treads on the road and told us that the tank had sighted us, turned around, and backed into a near-by village. "We're going to dig in here," he added, "and send out patrols to hunt him down."

But the tank didn't require any hunting. Even as we were entrenching in a graveyard flanking the main road, the enormous thing rumbled into view about fifteen hundred yards to our left. It was astraddle a railroad, and there was a second tank behind it. We had no idea how many more tanks might be in the little village that lay between us and Colonel Smith's battalion. And, to make things even more tense, Colonel Smith's battalion was now urgently messaging us for ammunition. Unless the tanks were smashed, his forward battalion would be cut off.

At this point a small ammunition-laden convoy roared up the road. Two lieutenants jumped out and rushed up the hill to Lieutenant Payne. They were tall, fine-looking officers with all the bravado and eagerness of very young, very green soldiers. One announced theatrically to Payne, "Charlie, our orders are to crash through with this ammunition and to hell with the sniper fire. We'll make it all right, but we'd like you to give us a couple of your men."

Somewhat owlishly, but in a voice that bespoke authority, Lieutenant Payne said, "Things are changing a bit. We'll just wait and make another check with headquarters. Then maybe we'll make like Custer."

Roy and I both smiled at that. We were becoming increasingly impressed with the sure, professional way Payne was handling the situation. I had asked him earlier in the day how he felt about being back at war.

"Well," he said, "when I learned in Japan that I was coming over here I was plain scared to death—I figured that I'd run through my share of good luck in Italy. A man's only got a certain number of close calls coming to him. But as soon as I heard the guns I got over it."

Payne would really have been worried if he had known just how very hard he was going to have to press his share of good luck. When I saw him again in August, he and Colonel Ayres were the only two survivors of the battalion headquarters staff of eleven. Of the battalion itself, about 900 men at full strength, only 263 were still on the line. The rest were wounded or dead.

From our graveyard foxholes we saw the first of these deaths—the first American death in Korea.

When orders to attack first went out to the fifty-odd youngsters in our bazooka team they gazed at the tanks as if they were watching a newsreel. It took prodding from their officers to make them realize that this was it—that it was up to them to attack. Slowly, small groups of them left their foxholes, creeping low through the wheat field toward the tank. The first swoosh from a bazooka flared out when they were nearly five hundred yards away from the tanks. But the aim was good and it looked like a direct hit.

But apparently it didn't look good to Lieutenant Payne. "Damn," he said, "those kids are scared—they've got to get close to the tanks to do any damage."

The first Communist tank whose turret rose above the protecting foliage along the railway answered the bazooka with a belch of flame. We could see enemy soldiers jump from the tank, and machine guns began to chatter at the approaching bazooka teams. Through my field glasses I could see a blond American head poke up out of the grass —the young soldier was trying to adjust his aim. Flashes from the tank flicked the ground horribly close, and I thought I saw him fall. It was so murky I wasn't sure. But in a few minutes I heard a soldier shout, "They got Shadrick—right in the chest. He's dead, I guess." The tone of voice was very matter-of-fact. I thought then how much more matter-of-fact the actuality of war is than any of its projections in literature. The wounded seldom cry—there's no one with time and emotion to listen.

Bazookas were still sounding off. We felt certain that the tanks, which were like sitting ducks astride the tracks, would be demolished within a matter of minutes. But time passed, and suddenly, after an hour, we saw the bazooka boys coming back toward us across the fields.

"My God," said Mydans, "they look as if the ball game was over and it's time to go home."

"What's going on?" I asked a sergeant.

"We ran out of ammo," he answered bitterly. "And the enemy infantry moving up way outnumbers us. Besides, these damn bazooks don't do any good against those heavy tanks—they bounce right off."

So, on the very first day of the war, we began to learn that the bazookas were no match for the Soviet tanks unless they scored a lucky hit from very close range. But even so it seemed incredible that we were going to pull back with enemy tanks still within our lines. I was gripped with a sense of unreality that followed me through most of the war. Reality, I guess, is just what we are accustomed to—and in Korea there was never time to become accustomed to anything.

Incredible or not, it was clear enough as we returned to the command post that we Americans had not only been soundly defeated in our first skirmish but that a major retreat of our battalion would be forced. We simply had nothing with which to halt the tanks, and we were far too few to prevent the North Korean infantry from coming around our flanks. We hated to think what was happening to Colonel Smith's forward battalion.

But you soon learn, at a war front, to place events firmly in separate emotional compartments. There was absolutely nothing to be gained by thinking about Colonel Smith's situation. When we got back to battalion headquarters I think most of us tried to lock the door of the worry compartment and concentrate on immediate, material problems.

This was fairly easy for me that day, for a very simple reason. My first act, on getting out of the jeep at head-quarters, was to slip and sprawl flat on my belly in a muddy rice paddy. Soaked and mud-caked, my consuming, immediate interest was the getting-dry department. °

Lieutenant Payne came to my rescue. He found me some dry green fatigues and gallantly escorted me to an empty thatched hut where I changed. Next on the list of compelling interests was flea powder. I had been in agony all day, completely defenseless against as vicious an assault as fleadom ever made. A thick network of bites pocked my waist, thighs, and ankles. I hurried down to the medic's hut to beg for the little gray box of insecticide powder which was to be my most precious personal possession of the Korean war.

I was talking to a Medical Corps sergeant when they brought in the body of Private Shadrick. His face was un-covered. As they carefully laid his body down on the bare boards of the shack I noticed that his face still bore an expression of slight surprise. It was an expression I was to see often among the soldier dead. The prospect of death had probably seemed as unreal to Private Shadrick as the entire war still seemed to me. He was very young indeed —his fair hair and frail build made him look far less than his nineteen years.

Someone went to look for a dry blanket for him, and just then the medic came back with the flea powder. He glanced at the body as he was handing me the gray box.

"What a place to die," he said.

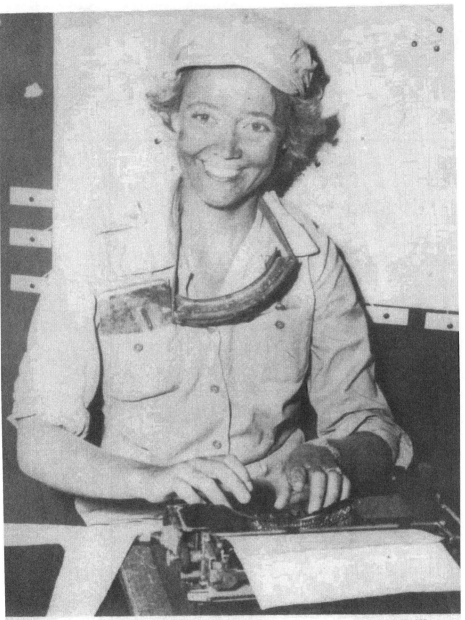

MYDANS

Marguerite Higgins at work on the manuscript for this book.

MYDANS

Refugee.

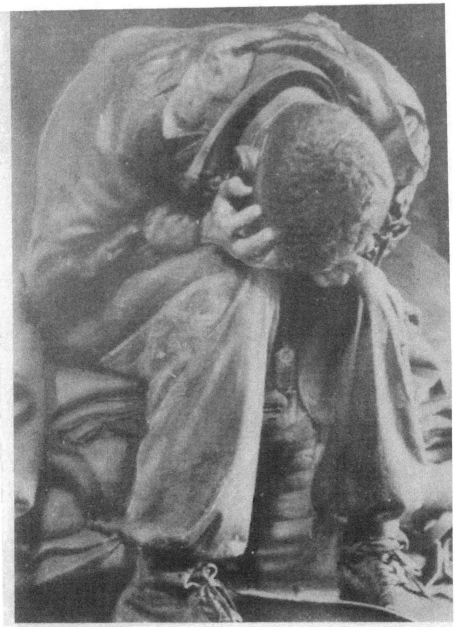

ACME

The wages of war.

General Douglas MacArthur and his political adviser, Brigadier
General Courtney Whitney, observe a paratroop jump.

ACME

War-weary GI limps back to his base.

Casualty.

A Korean family sets out to find a new home.

CHAPTER 5

"HOW FAST CAN AN ARMY RETREAT?"

The full impact of our first disaster in Korea hit General Barth's command post within eighteen hours of the opening skirmish.

The story unfolded shortly after midnight. I had been trying to sleep on a blanket-covered bit of floor where other correspondents and most of the battalion officers were also stretched out. Despite bone-aching weariness, the memory of our bazooka skirmish and the thought of tanks within our lines filled my brief sleep with uneasiness. Stealthy, unexplained stirrings in the room set my heart banging.

Suddenly through the darkness a voice whispered to me, "Better get into the war room fast. We may have to pull out suddenly."

In the hall I flashed a light on my watch. It was one

o'clock. "It's retreating time again," I said to Carl Mydans, who appeared in the darkness. As he looked at me questioningly, I added, "It's exactly the same time that we had to leave Seoul and Suwon."

We stepped quietly into the tense, hushed war room. In the center sat General Barth and "Red" Ayres. Deep concern had replaced the confidence that had marked both these men only twelve hours earlier.

A kerosene light flaring on the table in front of them highlighted their serious faces. The table was covered with a map and surrounded by field telephones. Separating the officers from the relentless downpour outside were grotesque rain-soaked blankets that flapped over the windows. The handful of correspondents stood in the darkness at the opposite end of the room.

Near us various officers were frantically grinding their field telephones, which cast strange shadows in the melodramatic light.

"This is danger forward. (Code name for our command post.) Trying to reach danger rear," one officer was saying urgently into the phone. Just as we entered, I saw three tattered, shaken GIs heading for the door. One was limping. They looked as if they had been on a prolonged Dunkerque.

"What's happening?" I asked Carl, who had been taking notes earlier as General Barth talked to the soldiers.

"It's the forward battalion," Carl answered. "These kids just escaped. They say most of the battalion is lost."

"Wait a minute," interjected General Barth. "These kids

are green and excited. We've just contacted an officer—Colonel Perry. Let's hear what he has to say."

In a few minutes Lieutenant Colonel Miller O. Perry appeared. He had difficulty walking. Shrapnel had got him in the leg. He walked slowly up to General Barth. His voice reflected a mixture of exhaustion and deep unhappiness.

"I'm sorry, sir," the colonel said simply. "We couldn't stop them. They came at us from all sides. We fired until we ran out of ammo."

Through the glare I could see General Barth pause a second. Then, with visible effort to take emotion out of his voice, he said, "I know that you and Colonel Smith did everything that could be done. How bad is it?"

"Bad, sir," Colonel Perry said. "We lost a lot of men."

"The wounded?"

"The litter cases were abandoned, sir."

The general winced and then asked in a very low voice, "Let's hear it briefly from the beginning."

"Right, sir," said Perry. "As you know, we were dug in north of the town of Osan on ridges on either side of the main road. We had some recoilless 75s, some mortars and other artillery. About eight-thirty in the morning those heavy tanks started rolling in on us. We took them under fire at about fifteen hundred yards and hit four or five. But we couldn't stop them—they rolled right by our positions.

"We sent the bazooka boys down, but their fire couldn't hurt that armor. Pretty soon the tanks got around to our rear and were shooting at our positions from behind. Then the infantry came in with automatic weapons and rifles. Some were dressed like farmers, in whites, and the rest had on mustard-colored uniforms. They came like flies, all around us.

"We had no way of protecting ourselves from encirclement. We didn't have enough men to deploy. Then we got caught in the cross fire of the tanks and infantry. We were out of rations and out of ammo by three in the afternoon. We had to leave all our heavy guns, though we took out the breeches. The last I saw of Colonel Smith, he was leading a group of men over the hill."

Superimpose Colonel Perry's story on a series of American holding positions southward and you have a picture of the Communist tactics for the major phases of the war. And the Chinese, when they came in, followed exactly the same battle procedures.

When not successfully spearheaded by tanks, enemy infantry would take advantage of our numerical weakness to infiltrate and encircle. I remember describing it in a story as a "circular front." Particularly in those early days, we were attacked from the rear and the sides as often as head on. We started the war with three under-strength battalions. They were perfect targets for the enemy battle plan.

As the war developed, the Communists perfected some new tricks, of course. As they captured more and more of our equipment, they began to disguise themselves in American uniforms and try to fool the troops by calling to them in English and pretending to be South Korean allies.

But the basic pattern never changed. The enemy simply avoided frontal assault and depended on infiltration and a series of enveloping movements.

Both the North Koreans and the Chinese keyed their tactics around their one big advantage—vast quantities of man power. And they were extravagant with it, as we learned that night from Colonel Perry. His phrase, "They came at us like flies," became a commonplace one in the next few months.

As the colonel finished his unhappy account, General Barth's first words were, "My God, to think I personally pulled away the dynamite from those bridges." It seemed that General Barth's confidence in Colonel Smith's ability to hold the line had been so great that the general had removed the materials with which the South Koreans planned to blow the bridges in the face of the oncoming tanks. Now there was absolutely nothing to stop them.

Our weak half-strength battalion was inevitably due for the next blow. We could not understand why the enemy had not struck already.

We didn't know it then, but there were six well-armed North Korean divisions bearing down on us. Why they did not push their tanks straight through to Pusan then and there is one of the war's mysteries. A hard push would have crumbled our defenses, as everyone from General MacArthur on down now concedes. Facing the enemy were only a thousand Americans at the most and the disorganized remnants of the South Koreans.

General MacArthur believes that the Communist hesitations in the opening weeks of the Korean war constitute their biggest mistake. They overestimated us as much as we underestimated them.

Knowing that our battalion was due for a showdown, I elected to stay on and watch the fight. General Barth offered both Carl and myself a ride back to the regiment, adding, "I'll bring you on back up here early in the morning." We accepted and rode off in General Barth's command car to Songhwan, some twenty miles south of Pyontek. The command post, as usual, was located in a schoolhouse. Regimental officers were bending over maps, grinding telephones, and frantically trying to piece together what was happening up front. As so often happened in this lightning-fast war, correspondents had to function as liaison officers. Carl and I were cross-examined at length about the bazooka skirmish, and we reported the situation in as much detail as we could remember.

It was now 3 A.M. With the waning of excitement, weariness closed in again. Until this period in the Korean war I had not realized that the bodily mechanism could be pushed so hard and so long without sleep. Later, watching soldiers and marines march miles and then fight all night and day without sleep, I realized what a comparatively small dosage of exhaustion we correspondents had to endure. But on that particular night the long, rough jeep ride in the cold, the innumerable hikes up and down hills, and the many previous nights with only an hour or two of sleep combined to put both Carl and myself in a state of stupor. Despite the hubbub around us, we each

.picked a rickety table top in the corner of the kerosene-lighted room, stretched out, and fell asleep.

When I woke at about 5:30 A.M.—I think the silence and a new crop of fleabites must have done it—there was not a single American soldier left in the room. Maps, guns, and the big square cases of C rations that had been strewn around the floor were gone.

Carl, his head propped on his elbow and his eyes still blurred with sleep, was blinking about the room with disbelief.

"Why, the whole damn regiment has moved right out from under us," he said. "How fast can an army retreat?"

There was nothing to do but go out to hitch a ride, wondering what new disaster had caused the sudden move.

CHAPTER **6**

"THE EARLY DAYS"

When we reached headquarters of the rapidly forming 24th Division at Taejon, we were told that the sudden retreat south of Pyontek had been a "mistake." General Barth asserted that we had way outrun the enemy and had given up ground needlessly.

I am continually astonished when, with the benefit of hindsight, I remember the atmosphere of confidence at division headquarters on that day. It was July fifth. The war was ten days and four retreats old. Major General William Dean, one of the kindliest and finest of soldiers, was just taking over the division command. In spite of what had happened, the myth persisted that just a few more soldiers and a few more guns could turn the tide. On that date, according to my notes, the newly appointed briefing officer estimated that it might take ten more days before we could mount a counteroffensive. I remember cabling my office, "Best headquarters estimate is a six- to eight-week war."

But sometime in the nightmare of the next few days headquarters realized our desperate peril. Then it became a fierce race to scrape together reinforcements and rush them to Korea.

To meet the danger, Japan was stripped of its American occupation troops. But still this was not enough. For we were terribly unprepared in the Far East. General Douglas MacArthur had repeatedly—and urgently—warned Washington that he had insufficient forces in the event of an emergency. Here was sad proof of his wisdom. Even at home America itself had fantastically few trained men on hand. In Korea regular army officers who knew the paucity of our numbers wondered if enough men could possibly be mustered. Then the United States, fighting under the banner of the United Nations, made the fateful decision to send virtually every mobilized American soldier to Korea, stripping our homeland of all but the most meager defenses. General Omar Bradley, Chairman of the Joint Chiefs of Staff, later told America the "bruising truth" of how deeply the Korean war bit into our supply of trained soldiers.

America paid heavily for its unpreparedness. It bought time with the lives of a few who were sacrificed against hopeless odds to hold till reinforcements should arrive. The swiftness with which reinforcements were rushed to the scene once the crisis was recognized is a tribute to the resourcefulness of the United States Army, Navy, and Air Force. It cannot make up for the men who are dead and who might at least have had a fighting chance to live had we been prepared.

Delaying action is the military term for the licking we took in those strange, faraway places: Chonan, Chonui, Chochiwon, the Kum River, Taejon, Yongdong Po—a saddening litany for anyone who witnessed those frightful days in Korea.

At Chonan—the first of these holding actions—the enemy caught us in a deadly trap. We walked into it in the effort to regain the ground that headquarters believed had been needlessly relinquished in the last swift retreat.

Our jeepload of correspondents accompanied the reinforced American patrol on its excursion into no man's land. Keyes, back from Tokyo, was at the wheel, and the old team—Tom Lambert, Roy McCartney, Carl Mydans, and myself—was together again.

The patrol was led by Major Boone Seegars, a tall, smooth-looking officer of an almost Arrow-shirt-advertisement quality of handsomeness. I had met him briefly in Germany, my previous post. There Major Seegars, a World War II pilot, had functioned as the aide of General Joseph T. McNarney, onetime commander-in-chief in Germany.

"I transferred out of the Air Force at my mother's request," Major Seegars explained as we started out. "You see, I'm an only child, and she was terribly worried about me in the last war." The major paused a second then and added wryly, "So now I'm leading a patrol."

We tucked in behind the radio jeep. Two infantry platoons marched in ditches by the sides of the road and heavy guns were all set to roll forward if we needed them.

After several miles we spotted the enemy dug in ahead of us. To our surprise, the enemy soldiers hurriedly withdrew over the brow of the hill at our approach. An eager first lieutenant said, "Let's hurry them up with some fire."

But Major Seegars thought differently. "We have plenty of time," he said. "Let's see how far we can make them run without firing a shot."

The North Korean Reds scurried away from hilltop after hilltop for about six hours as we cautiously probed forward. We rode through Chonan without drawing a shot, its rickety wooden houses deserted and silent.

Suddenly our caravan stopped. Rifle fire struck at us from the hill ahead and a few mortars lobbed in. But resistance was slight and soon ebbed. However, Major Seegars decided to pause and call up the artillery.

At this point—four o'clock in the afternoon—Keyes urged that it was time to go back and file our stories. Copy was log-jammed back at Taejon and there was as much as twenty hours' delay. I was in a spot. I hated to leave the situation at this critical juncture. But if I pressed the time too close, I might miss my deadline altogether. There was the transportation problem, too, and Keyes was the boss of that jeep. So I decided to head back to Taejon, about a two-and-a-half-hour ride.

Pausing at the 34th Infantry Regimental Command, I found new cause for worry. It seemed that in the brief period since we had left the forward patrol a skirmish had been reported. Then communications had broken down.

When we heard this, Keyes and I decided that we would not even attempt to get any sleep that night at headquarters, but would head straight back to the front the moment our stories had been telephoned.

Twelve hours later dawn was breaking as we finally got back to the fighting lines. By that time Major Seegars was dead. His patrol and the battalion that had gone to the rescue had been ambushed in a sanguinary battle that had raged all night in and around Chonan. The command of the 34th Regiment had changed twice. The first commander had been relieved, and the second, Colonel Martin, had died attacking a tank with a bazooka from fifteen yards.

"Blew him right in half," said Captain Eugene Healey, whom we met there on the road. "A real tough guy, but he only lasted a few hours."

Smoke and colored flares spiraled out of Chonan as American artillery poured it on. They were trying to smash the oncoming advance of the Communist tanks and give cover to retreating GIs. The exhausted doughboys came straggling around the bend, hungry, bedraggled, and disgusted.

Red shells started zeroing in as we stood there, and about ten of the infantrymen jumped on the jeep as Keyes zoomed down the road.

"For Christ sakes, get down, I can't see," he yelled to the GIs on the radiator. A shell burst close, and a GI on the hood, his face cut by the fragments, yelled frantically, "Get going, will you."

Once a safe distance from the shells, Keyes and I tried to take stock. Soon our stories of the patrol would be telephoned to Tokyo for transmission to the United States. Under ordinary circumstances I would still have had time to rush back to communications and catch the story—now so completely changed—before my deadline.

Keyes, reading my thoughts, shook his head. "You've had it. That filing system has you licked." I realized he was right. For at Taejon each piece of copy was given a place in line to be telephoned and you could make no substitutions. According to the system, I could not remove my story of the successful patrol and submit instead the story of the Chonan debacle. The new development would have to take its place in line, and because of the pile-up of copy it would be another twenty-four hours before it would get out. The news agencies were in the same spot as I was. And that is why the dispatches featuring Major Boone Seegars as the enthusiastic leader of America's first successful patrol continued to appear all over the United States for hours after we all knew that he had died a heroic death.

We asked Captain Healey, who had joined us, to tell us about Chonan.

"The gooks really trapped us," he said. "They let us through the town, then came at us from the hills and from the rear. Those tanks must have been there all the time, hidden behind these deserted-looking houses. We got lots of them, but you can't get a tank with a carbine."

(American tanks arrived just too late to take part in the fight for Chonan.)

This was the prelude to a seemingly endless series of retreats. In the coming days I saw war turn many of our young soldiers into savagely bitter men. I saw young Americans turn and bolt in battle, or throw down their arms cursing their government for what they thought was embroilment in a hopeless cause. But I was also to see other young boys perform incredibly brave deeds to save a position, help a buddy, or, more simply, to live up to their belief that, as citizens of a great nation, they had a duty to fight well.

Most correspondents in Korea would report, I think, that it pays off to expect much of an American. Outfits like the Marines and the 27th (Wolfhound) Infantry Regiment wanted to justify the publicity about them. They knew they were supposed to be good. And each individual was damned if he was going to do anything to disprove the theory. They were prodded on by their own collective good opinion of themselves. Sometimes this is called *esprit de corps*. But people like Lieutenant Ray Murray of the 5th Marines simply say "Gallant, hell. These guys fight well because they don't want to let the rest of the guys down. And the rest of the guys have pretty high standards."

The standards of discipline were quite understandably low in the weeks of defeat. Any human being wants a fighting chance. You don't get that at fifty-to-one odds. In the first skirmishes in Korea we paid a high price in the lives of trained officers because a disturbing number of our troops were reluctant to follow orders to stand fast. It was routine to hear comments like, "Just give me a jeep and I know which direction I'll go in. This mamma's boy ain't cut out to be no hero," or, "Someone really gave old Harry the wrong dope on this war. He can find someone else to pin his medals on."

It was hard to impress the average GI with the fact that these successive holding actions in Korea were the best that America could do under the circumstances and that these sacrifices were gaining us desperately needed time.

These arguments are a mockery if you have just seen your men massacred in what seems a hopeless fight. Lieutenant Edward James, twenty-five years old, who had crawled down a river bed to safety after having held "at any cost," approached me in a fury. As his lips trembled with exhaustion and anger, he said, "Are you correspondents telling the people back home the truth? Are you telling them that out of one platoon of twenty men, we have three left? Are you telling them that we have nothing to fight with, and that it is an utterly useless war?"

Many high-ranking Americans who should never have taken a chance in the front lines had to go forward to steady the soldiers by their example. One of these was Colonel Richard Stephens, of the 21st Infantry Regiment, who won a silver star for directing one of the first battles from a forward outpost. The regimental commander was the last to leave his position.

He described the situation this way: "The boys had to

stick around this time, what with all the high-priced help",
—meaning himself—"around."

Colonel Stephens added that he decided his presence at
company level was necessary because "before when I
said 'Withdraw,' these boys would just take off like a big
bird. And panic—taking off every which way, dropping
your weapons and such—gets too many people killed."

In the first three weeks of the war I was filled with pity
at the sense of betrayal—and astonishment—displayed by
our young soldiers who had been plucked so suddenly out
of the soft occupation life in Japan and plunged into battle. Most had had only routine basic training and were far
from combat ready. Only a small percentage had ever
heard artillery fire before.

Americans do like to go soft between wars, and hereto-
fore we have always been able to afford that luxury. In
Korea, America found out it could never let down until a
showdown—military or diplomatic—with the Soviet-dic-
tated world brings some kind of reliable international
truce. Somehow American leadership is going to have to
impress on every potential GI that there are strong odds
that he's going to have to fight some dirty battles to keep
the vanilla-ice-cream kind of world he has been brought
up in. Korea showed that we had fallen miserably short in
indoctrinating the GIs. The United States, which may one
day have a much more important war on its hands, should
face this fact squarely. Otherwise it will continue to find
in its ranks soldiers reluctant to fight. And we can no
longer risk the loss of life that comes when you toss troops

that are unprepared psychologically and physically into the kind of combat imposed by the Communists and their satellites.

It was fascinating in Korea to watch the changing attitudes in our front-line soldiers. If, by the end of August, you asked any front-line GI what he was fighting for, he felt—because most GIs aren't very articulate—just as embarrassed at the question as he had been three months before. But the things he was saying around the front to his buddies and the stubbornness he displayed in combat showed that he was gradually understanding that this system he was fighting was an ugly, threatening thing and that it was best to beat it as far from his own shores as possible.

A lot of things could have brought about this change: a look at the bodies of American prisoners, their hands tied behind their backs with white engineer tape, murdered in cold blood; a conversation with an English-speaking Korean refugee who could tell firsthand about life in the Red-occupied north; the absurd name-calling propaganda of Seoul City Sue. Whatever the cause, it was encouraging to see the change.

More impressive than the bitterness was the utter resignation with which some of the officers, like Colonel Ayres, faced the succession of debacles. I remember visiting his battalion several days after Chonan. Ayres's outfit had been going through some hell of its own west of Chonan. But they had pulled back finally out of contact with the enemy. In the lull, depression and tiredness spread.

Ayres asked Mydans, "Have you heard anything more about American troops arriving?"

"No," answered Mydans unhappily. "I wish I did have some good news for you. Have you any special reason for asking?"

"Oh no," responded Ayres. "I was just kind of wondering if any more Americans were coming, and if they were, whether we'd be still around to see them."

During those terrible days, the North Korean Reds had three key advantages. First, they had overwhelming superiority of man power, which often saw our soldiers fighting against ten-, twenty-, and even fifty-to-one odds. Time after time companies would tell of night infiltrations through their lines by Communists who would suddenly appear at dawn on top of their foxholes at the ratio of five or ten to every GI.

Secondly, the Commies had heavy tanks which we were unable to halt effectively until the third week of the war, when rocket launchers were brought in.

Our own light tanks were no match for Soviet armor under ordinary circumstances, and our officers refused to commit them in tank battles except in case of dire emergency. (American tanks then mounted 75-millimeter guns, whereas the Soviets were 88-millimeter, even 90-millimeter.)

Soviet tank superiority was brought home to me vividly one day on a curving mountain road, where a bitter young infantry sergeant, leading a platoon in a counterattack, complained, "Them American tanks run out on us the minute they heard the Russian babies coming round the corner."

The sergeant added disgustedly, "I asked the tank commander where the hell he thought he was going. He had the nerve to tell me he was heading back because his tank was at an unfair disadvantage against Russian armor. I asked that slob what sort of armor he thought I had on my back."

North Koreans had far more tanks available than had been estimated—more than four hundred in initial stages of combat alone, as compared to sixty-five predicted by intelligence. And the successful tank-spearheaded advance of North Korean infantry taught us that, in mountainous terrain, air superiority cannot possibly be relied on to neutralize enemy armor.

This is not to belittle either air-force or marine tactical aviation. I've seen the murderous effects of a rocket-launching plane-strike on Soviet tanks—charred bits of steel and flesh blown hundreds of yards.

But ask any veteran officers of the Korean campaign and he'll tell you that the best answer to massed enemy tanks is bigger and better masses of American tanks. By early fall American 47½-ton Patton tanks were in action in substantial numbers and had scored victories against the 38-ton Soviet T-34.

Any GI reminiscing over the first days of the Korean war will remember with grimness how many felt that the swift-jet planes were more of a hindrance than a help. During the first four days of battle I was forward with battalions which were strafed every day by our own jets. Dug in a ditch with jets swooshing rockets that seemed personally aimed at us, a GI, on the second day of the war, summed up the general feeling with the remark, "Why don't those jet guys either stay at thirty thousand feet or go back to the officers' club?"

But those were the opening days. The improvement in air-ground co-ordination techniques was miraculous. There was nothing wrong with air-force tactical procedures that an incredibly brief amount of practice didn't improve. Having been one of the first to write about the poor air-ground co-ordination, I feel compelled to say that in light of the full record the accent of publicity has, in my opinion, been unfair. I shall never forget those strafings, but I shall never forget either how, on the seventh day of the war, a sergeant watching Mustangs diving at targets only a few hundred yards away commented admiringly, "Those guys ought to have bayonets on their propellers."

The Communists had the third great advantage of confusion, especially the confusion caused by the difficulty our troops had in distinguishing the North Korean foe from the South Korean friend. The Reds made the most of it. Time after time an American soldier would pass an innocent-looking bearded Korean farmer hoeing a rice paddy only to be confronted with the same figure throwing grenades at him in a dawn attack. In engagements with our Negro troops, Communists went so far as to black their faces with charcoal and don the uniforms stripped from dead or wounded Americans. So disguised, they managed to walk right up on our positions.

Then there were the streams of refugee women with huge bundles on their heads, babies on their backs, old men equally bent and weighted, and droves of children. We soon learned to suspect them. Many escaped American prisoners warned of seeing bent old Korean men and women "refugees" appear at Red outposts, and produce mortar plates and guns from otherwise innocuous-seeming bundles.

Add to all this the inevitable disorder of troops overrun, nipped off unit by unit, and constantly on retreat, and you can picture the wild atmosphere surrounding our outnumbered young soldiers. A sergeant of Red Ayres's battalion plaintively expressed the situation one day with the remark, "Nobody knows where we are except the North Koreans."

So, all considered, it is nothing short of miraculous that the officers, commissioned and non-commissioned, of the 24th Infantry Division were able to pull together their green, bewildered troops and successfully hold off the enemy as long as they did. They did wonders with the peacetime occupation army that had never expected combat, and certainly not under those conditions. Rarely in American history have so few been asked to do so much with so little.

The battle for Taejon, a key communications city, was the most critical and the most costly of the early-holding actions.

"We desperately needed," said General MacArthur, "the six days between July twelfth and eighteenth. And General Dean and his men won them for us."

It was in that period that the 1st Cavalry and the 25th Infantry Division were landed in Korea.

The price of Taejon was high. General Dean, a big, young-looking man of fifty with a wide, soft smile, had the terrible responsibility of ordering unit after unit to hold at any cost. I remember the sorrow with which he told a number of us, "The officers are wonderful. Why, I know of one lieutenant colonel who alone killed fifteen enemy with hand grenades. But I'm losing them all. Where am I going to get replacements?"

General Dean was one of his own replacements. It is legend now how he led five tanks through no man's land to a fiery roadblock to rescue his old friend, Colonel Melloy of the 19th Infantry Regiment; how he personally fired bazookas destroying enemy tanks; and how, after being wounded, he kept right on rounding up stragglers to guide their escape after enemy encirclement of Taejon made further defense futile.

At Taejon we tasted the full poison of North Korean cruelty. For Captain Lincoln J. Buttery, Medical Corpsman, it is a story spelled out in terms of a hillside massacre of a band of helpless wounded near the roadblock on Taejon road. Captain Buttery crawled away from the scene on his belly, dragging a wounded leg. He told me his tale in the stench and darkness of a filthy, bug-ridden hospital train bearing the wounded who had escaped the battle lines.

"About a dozen walking wounded and an equal number of litter patients were trapped north of the roadblock last night," Captain Buttery began. "The Catholic chaplain, Father Hermann Feldhoelter, and the Protestant chaplain, Captain Kenneth Hyslop, and I were the officers with them. Father Feldhoelter told the walking wounded to take to the hills and make out as best they could. Those in better condition stayed behind to help us carry the litter patients.

"But the terrain was rough. About midnight we ran into trouble. Those burp guns rattled at us. We put the litters down and tried to take cover. Captain Hyslop and Father Feldhoelter paid no attention to the fire. Father Feldhoelter went from litter to litter administering last rites. Men were dying. Pretty soon Captain Hyslop got nicked.

"We could hear the Koreans yelling and carrying on, the way they do. We knew they would be on top of us soon.

"Father Feldhoelter said to me and the Protestant chaplain—the rest of the litter bearers had left—'You two must leave. You have families and responsibilities. Mine is the duty to stay.'

"I started crawling away as it got light. I glanced back as I slipped over the bluff. The Reds—young kids sixteen to eighteen, they looked—were closing in. The litter patients screamed and screamed, 'No, no!' but the Reds shot them anyway. Father Feldhoelter was kneeling by one of the stretchers. He made no sound as he fell."

CHAPTER 7

NEWSMAN HIGGINS

In the midst of the battle of Taejon, I received a personal blow that rocked me as rudely as if it had been a bullet. I received orders to get out of the Korean theater of war immediately. No one, including the officer who passed the message on to me, knew why.

Everyone jumped to the conclusion that I, like Tom Lambert of Associated Press and Pete Kalischer of the United Press, had been accused of writing stories "giving aid and comfort to the enemy."

In those weeks of defeat it was an agonizing period, emotionally and mentally, for front-line correspondents. We felt it our responsibility to report the disasters as we saw them. And we knew how passionately the guys who were doing the fighting wanted the "folks back home" to know what they were up against. But we frequently found ourselves called traitors by the brass at division, and especially the brass in Tokyo, for telling the brutal story about the licking our troops were taking.

I'd like to stress that there was never any quarrel between the press and officialdom on questions of purely military security. We were eager to keep out names of towns, camouflage tactical maneuvers, and, in short, cooperate in depriving the enemy of any information that might be of military help to him. We repeatedly asked, without success, for military censorship so that we would have uniform guidance. If we slipped—and I know I did in the first few days—it was because of ignorance or confusion. (Censorship was finally imposed seven months later. And then it went way beyond my concept of military censorship; in my opinion, it added up to psychological and political censorship.)

But in those early days officialdom's quarrel with us was over our reports on the bitterness and greenness of our troops and the humiliating mauling they were taking. Aside from accusing us of disloyalty, MacArthur's officialdom had the very real weapon of being able to throw us out summarily if we displeased them.

Like most newsmen, I deeply believe this: so long as our government requires the backing of an aroused and informed public opinion, so long as we are a democracy, it is necessary to tell the hard "bruising truth." It is best to admit panic among our soldiers and so bring home the great need for better training; it is best to admit that bazookas don't even tickle the big Soviet tanks and make

Miss Higgins and fellow correspondents at a front-line observation post.

Miss Higgins and Carl Mydans.

An American infantryman whose buddy has just been killed is comforted by a fellow soldier.

MYDANS

A wounded American soldier being carried from a jeep.

Near Taejon an American infantryman winces with pain as corps-
men break the hold of a wounded buddy.

known the urgent need for better and more weapons; it
is best to tell graphically the moments of desperation and
horror endured by an unprepared army, so that the American public will demand that it not happen again.

With these convictions, I and the rest of my colleagues
quoted the Captain Healeys of the war ("You can't get
a tank with a carbine"); told of the "whipped and fright-
ened" GIs; took our rebukes; and hoped that officialdom's
bark was worse than its bite.

But, as it turned out, my stories had nothing to do with
my banishment. I was being thrown out on orders of
Lieutenant General Walton H. Walker because I was a
female and because "there are no facilities for ladies at
the front."

The banishment-from-Korea edict came as very much
of a last straw in what had been a frantic period, not just
for me but for all correspondents. We never had any com-
plaints about obtaining chow or a place to sleep; we
could always scrounge for ourselves. The big hurdle was
coping with headquarters and somehow, despite officialdom, getting the story out. We had, as a press corps, almost no co-operation in obtaining two essentials to our
trade as war correspondents: transportation and communications. Keyes and I were the envy of the group because of our jeep, the one he had rescued from Seoul. For
many months we had the only available vehicle. The rest
of the press usually hitchhiked. Even during the brief
days of victory it was easier to get a jeep out of the South
Koreans, with their pitifully few vehicles, than from the

Eighth Army, which had motor pools gorged with jeeps.

Despite the much-publicized 270 accreditations to the Korean war, there were never to my knowledge more than sixty-odd correspondents actually at the front at any one time, and the average was closer to twenty.

Hal Boyle, Associated Press columnist, whose long experience in World War II puts him in a better position to speak than I, said, "Never since, and including, the Civil War have correspondents had so few of the facilities vital to their trade."

Colonel Pat Echols, MacArthur's press chief, apparently regarded the press as natural enemies. He couldn't get rid of us completely, but he could make our reporting life very difficult. This headquarters attitude inevitably was reflected by the Army in Korea. The Air Force and the Marines, on the other hand, took the view, "Once our official business is clear, we'll give you what help we can." And that's all anyone asked.

One early rule that made us particularly angry was that the telephone could be used only from 12 to 4 A.M. or from 2 to 4 A.M. It didn't matter whether the line was completely free of military traffic at other hours; the arbitrary twelve-to-four rule would stick until another rule came along. We resented the drain on our energies made by what we viewed as unnecessary difficulties. We felt that the first call on our time should be coverage of the troops at the front.

At Taejon there had been crisis after crisis. The Army had cut off telephones again, and a new backlog meant that the only way to get a story out was to fly it personally to Japan.

Also, despite friendly reassurances from Keyes and Carl and Roy, I was sincerely worried about my job. I had heard nothing from the office since my colleague's warning that I would be fired if I stayed on in Korea. My state of mind was shaky and there was a continual, oppressive lump in the worry department located in my midriff.

So, as usual with bad things, the banishment edict could not have come at a worse time. I felt, of course, that it was highly unjust, and warranted a direct appeal to General MacArthur.

I had already been with the troops three weeks. Now, with an entire division in the line and more due to arrive, the worst had already been endured. Realizing that as a female I was an obvious target for comment, I had taken great pains not to ask for anything that could possibly be construed as a special favor. Like the rest of the correspondents, when not sleeping on the ground at the front with an individual unit, I usually occupied a table top in the big, sprawling room at Taejon from which we telephoned. The custom was to come back from the front, bang out your story, and stretch out on the table top. You would try to sleep, despite the noise of other stories being shouted into the phone, till your turn came to read your story to Tokyo. Then, no matter what the hour, you would probably start out again because the front lines were changing so fast you could not risk staying away any longer than necessary.

As for "facilities for ladies"—a euphemism employed by generals when they want to be delicate about latrines— nobody in Korea, including the Koreans, worried much about powder rooms. There is no shortage of bushes in Korea.

Bad language? Well, I'd already been at the front in World War II. And I really didn't need a trip to our front lines to know how to fill in the dots and dashes in Hemingway's novels. The American Swearing Vocabulary is pretty limited, so far as I've observed. Nor do I think I inhibited the soldiers much, at least not much more than to make them lower their voices now and again. The niceties of language on a battle front just don't seem very important.

I telephoned General Walker in Taegu, and pleaded at the very least not to be yanked out of the story till a replacement could arrive. (My *Herald Tribune* colleague was then at sea to cover the 1st Cavalry's amphibious landing.) It was unfair, I argued, to deprive the *Herald Tribune* of coverage at this critical juncture in the Taejon battle. The answer was, "You'll have to leave." I told Walker I'd go "as soon as feasible."

On the afternoon of the edict a major tried to put me on the train leaving Taejon. But I had been entrusted by Keyes (also on the amphibious landing) with the jeep and was determined not to be separated from it. General Dean supported me in this, arguing that there was no need, after so many weeks of war, to give me a "bum's rush."

From then on, with my appeal to MacArthur still up in the air, I simply avoided headquarters and stayed at the front. In the succeeding days, rumor of my plight soon got around. A touching number of soldiers, from regimental commanders to privates first class, took the trouble to come to me and say, "We hope you can talk the general out of this." I believe they were sincere.

Their concern made me feel awful. There is very little that is not wasteful and dismal about war. The only clear, deep, good is the special kind of bond welded between people who, having mutually shared a crisis, whether it be a shelling or a machine-gun attack, emerge knowing that those involved behaved well. There is much pretense in our everyday life, and, with a skillful manner, much can be concealed. But with a shell whistling at you there is not much time to pretend and a person's qualities are starkly revealed. You believe that you can trust what you have seen. It is a feeling that makes old soldiers, old sailors, old airmen, and even old war correspondents, humanly close in a way shut off to people who have not shared the same thing. I think that correspondents, because they are rarely in a spot where their personal strength or cowardice can affect the life of another, probably feel only an approximation of this bond. So far as I am concerned, even this approximation is one of the few emotions about which I would say, "It's as close to being absolutely good as anything I know."

As more and more old front-line friends commiserated with me, I was increasingly aware of the feeling of kinship and of my emotional involvement in the war. It made the prospect of departure all the harder. The Reds had thrown me out of Seoul and it had been a long walk out. I wanted terribly to stick with this man's Army till we all walked back in. I was very much pleased one day when Colonel Stephens, trying to cheer me up, solemnly said, "I tell you what, Maggie, if they really try to throw you out as a correspondent, I'll hire you back for my rifle platoon."

Forty hours went by and still nothing from MacArthur. But there was one bright spot. My home office cabled that it was making strenuous efforts on my behalf. I was pleased and relieved. Their message was the first word since their original instructions to head for Korea, and it meant they supported me in my desire to stay at the front. It was one load off my mind.

By this time, July sixteenth, Taejon was tottering and almost all the rest of the correspondents had gone south with division rear echelon. I realized that a reversal of the edict apparently wasn't coming as quickly as I had hoped. The business of constantly dodging headquarters officialdom was very uncomfortable indeed. I decided to write my final front-line story and gradually go southward to Taegu. There I could plead my case personally with General Walker, who had said on the telephone that he would be glad to see me on my way through to Tokyo.

It looked that afternoon, for a few brief moments, as if I would never leave Taejon. Late in the day I was jeeping unconcernedly past the compound that enclosed division headquarters. Suddenly a roar of voices boomed to me to come back.

Looking back, I saw dozens of soldiers, their guns pointed in my direction, peeping around the compound fence. Tanks in front of headquarters also had their guns trained my way. So I hastily wheeled my jeep about and pell-melled into the compound, heading for the building we had adopted for the press. It was deserted except for Bill Smith of the London *Daily Express*.

"You got here just in time for some excitement," Smitty said. "Everybody is shooting, but nobody knows why or at what."

Smitty and I went over to the headquarters building to try to find out the cause of the trouble. But about all we found was a number of headquarters men, who had never been shot at before, under a table. Outside we found General Dean. He was leaning over the fence, the boards of which had just been nicked by bullets.

"Somebody is a bad shot," Dean said with a smile. "They should have got me that time."

One of the general's assistants suggested that maybe some of our own trigger-happy lads had started this thing and now we were all shooting at each other. As we looked around at troops firing aimlessly, we were inclined to agree. In any event, it was getting dark and we could not put off leaving the compound much longer. Our exit from town was practically jet-propelled. Smitty, convinced that the guerillas were imaginary, told me as we left the compound, "Now wave nicely at those tank boys, so that at least they won't shoot at us."

Smitty then stepped on the gas and we whizzed down the deserted main road through the town. To top off everything, our jeep, just at that critical moment, had an extreme seizure of backfiring, so that we sort of exploded down main street. If anyone fired at us, we never knew it. Our jeep outgunned them.

Joining the sad, dusty American exodus over the winding mountain road, we finally turned off at 21st Infantry Regimental Headquarters, located in a Korean schoolhouse. It was close to midnight and already the main room was filled with snoring officers sprawled on the floor. Everyone slept in his clothes for the simple reason that you had to be ready to move at a second's notice. I quietly put my blanket down on the floor, doused myself thoroughly with flea powder, and went to sleep.

The astonished officer who woke up the next morning and found me next to him on the floor caused considerable amusement around headquarters by dashing into Colonel Stephens's room with the exclamation, "My God, sir, did you know we'd been sleeping all night with a lady?"

The 21st Infantry, which had been badly cut up in previous fighting, was busy that day digging in for the inevitable battle that would come when the two battalions now defending Taejon were pressed back. I noticed that the soldiers seemed much calmer than in the days north of the Kum River. They were even wisecracking a lot.

One GI called out to me, "Hey, Maggie, look at this

foxhole I'm digging. I'm going to stop just short of where they'd get me for desertion."

"Yours is nothin'," chimed in his pal. "I'm diggin' me a real Hollywood foxhole. All the comforts."

I mentioned the change to Colonel Stephens.

"I told you," Stephens replied, "no American division is any damn good until after its first fight. These kids'll be okay after a while."

That night I started for Taegu on a "hospital train" which consisted of unlit, filthy Korean passenger cars. I had wanted to take the jeep, but it developed that the Eighth Army was in an extra big hurry to get me out of the country. The train was due to leave at midnight.

It seemed we waited there for hours in that hot, stinking car as ambulance after ambulance disgorged its load of wounded. Silent and sullen, the litter patients and the walking wounded were crowded into the gloomy train. They were in the charge of a medic corporal. Stretchers were placed across the backs of the wooden benches. A gangrenous odor of untended wounds mingled with the car's own smell—that of a very old latrine. Many of the wounded tried to lie down on the floor and on the wooden seats. But we were so crowded there was no way for anyone to stretch out. The heat and fetid air made me agonizingly sleepy.

In the car, the bitterness in the face of the young boy across from me was such that I almost hesitated to speak to him. His misery gave me a deep sense of guilt that I was not wounded. I wanted to say, "Look, I'm not here because I want to be, but because a three-star general insisted on putting me on this train." Finally I said, "Could I get you some water?"

The kid—he must have been about eighteen—said, "No, ma'am." Then he asked the question I had heard all around the front: "How come you're up here if you don't have to be?"

I explained that I was a war correspondent, that this was a tremendous story in the United States, and that people wanted to know from firsthand observers how the GIs were doing.

"I hope you are telling them that this is nothing more than a perpetual Battle of the Bulge," he said.

A sergeant across the way, whose leg had been amputated, broke in, "Oh, for God's sake, quit griping. We finally won the Bulge battle, didn't we?"

Two wounded died that night. But they made no sound. I learned of it only on reaching Taegu, where the train paused en route to Pusan and their bodies were carried off.

At Eighth Army, I went straight to General Walker's aide, to ask for a date to see the general. He said Walker was at the front but that I could probably catch him around three that afternoon.

As I was very sleepy, I inquired of a military policeman about the newly established Eighth Army correspondents' billet and was referred to a captain of public relations, a rather tall, square-shouldered young man.

He greeted me with, "You're not going to any correspondents' billet. I'm taking you to the airstrip, and right now, if I have to call some military police. And you can write that down in your little notebook [which I did]. I know all about you. You're just trying to make some unpleasant publicity for the general."

"Am I under arrest?" I asked.

"Don't pull that stuff," he replied. "I know your publicity tricks. The general's orders are to take you to the airstrip, under escort, if necessary."

"Look," I said, "I came here to see General Walker. All I want is his okay to go back to the front. I've got a tentative date to see him after three."

"You're not going to see anyone," was the answer. "You're going to the airstrip."

It wasn't hard to figure out that there was no use arguing. I wrote a note to the head PIO protesting the expulsion, and that was that. Then the captain called a jeep and armed himself with a carbine. Two similarly armed soldiers joined us, and off we went. On the way to the field he further clarified his views on women correspondents.

When I arrived in Tokyo that night I learned that General MacArthur had rescinded the expulsion order some twelve hours earlier. It must have been just about the time the captain was packing me off to the field.

Responding to a cable from Mrs. Ogden Reid, president of the New York *Herald Tribune,* MacArthur messaged: "Ban on women in Korea being lifted. Marguerite Higgins held in highest professional esteem by everyone." It was a very welcome change.

I've been asked a lot about the advantages and disadvantages of being a woman in my profession, especially in a war. I think the biggest disadvantage is that you are a target for all sorts of stories, most just exasperating, but some very vicious. The fact that they are untrue has nothing to do with quashing them. You just have to toughen the area between your shoulder blades and prepare for a lot of darts thrown in that direction.

Each time I'd go back to Tokyo, Carl would fill me in on the latest crop of Maggie Higgins stories. Once, very discouraged, I complained bitterly about them to Jimmy Cannon, columnist for the New York *Post*.

He said, "If the *Racing Form* sent a race horse to cover the war, he wouldn't be any more of an oddity than you are. That horse's activities would be the subject of all sorts of stories, and nobody would care how true they were so long as they were good stories. You're in the same fix and you'd better just quit worrying about what you hear."

I think Jimmy's advice was exactly right.

If you offer any competition in the highly competitive daily newspaper world, some male colleague—especially if he had just got a "where were you?" from his home office on one of your stories—is going to say that you got that story only because you have a very nice smile. Even if you got the information from the boss's female secretary and not from the boss, there is nothing you can do about it.

Some of the men correspondents in Korea had a distinct objection to female invasion of the field of war corresponding. Walter Simmons of the Chicago *Tribune* wrote in a news article, "Women correspondents in Korea are about as popular as fleas." This hostility was certainly shared at first by others, especially at the opening of the war. But it was never manifested in anything other than a few nasty comments now and again, and these came mainly from the Tokyo contingent rather than from the front-line correspondents.

At the actual war front a woman has equal competitive opportunities. Essentially it comes down to being in the combat area at the crucial time and having the stamina to do the jeeping and hiking necessary to get to where you can file your story.

Of course GIs whistle and wolf-call as you jeep past a convoy on a road. But when the shelling and the shooting starts, nobody pays any attention. They are too busy fighting and dodging bullets. No one has offered me his foxhole yet. And they didn't have to. I early developed a quick eye for protective terrain and can probably hit a ditch as fast as any man.

I recently received from Barry Bingham, president of the Louisville *Courier-Journal*, a clipping about me from his editorial page. It said, in part: "Miss Higgins shows no desire to win a name as a woman who dares to write at the spot where men are fighting. Her ambition is to be recognized as a good reporter, sex undesignated . . . An envelope in our newspaper library's clipping file is labeled: Higgins, Marguerite—Newsman. We believe Miss Higgins would like that."

The Louisville *Courier-Journal* was very right.

CHAPTER **8**

"STAND OR DIE"

I met the Eighth Army commander, Lieutenant General Walton H. Walker, for the first time when I returned to the front in mid-July after MacArthur had lifted the ban on women correspondents in Korea. General Walker was a short, stubby man of bulldog expression and defiant stance. I wondered if he were trying to imitate the late General George Patton, under whom he served in World War II as a corps commander.

He was very much of a spit-and-polish general, his lacquered helmet gleaming and the convoy of jeeps that escorted him always trim and shiny. I shall never forget the expression on the faces of two United States marine lieutenants who, on driving up to the Eighth Army compound at Seoul, were told by the military policeman at the gate: "You can't drive that vehicle in here. It's too dusty. No dusty jeeps in here. General Walker's orders!"

"Well, I'll be damned," breathed the marine lieutenant with deliberately exaggerated astonishment. "Everything we've been saying about the United States Army *is* true."

General Walker was very correct and absolutely frank with me.

He said he still felt that the front was no place for a woman, but that orders were orders and that from now on I could be assured of absolutely equal treatment.

"If something had happened to you, an American woman," the general explained, "I would have gotten a terrible press. The American public might never have forgiven me. So please be careful and don't get yourself killed or captured."

General Walker kept his promise of equal treatment, and from then on, so far as the United States Army was concerned, I went about my job with no more hindrance than the men.

Despite large-scale reinforcements, our troops were still falling back fast. Our lines made a large semicircle around the city of Taegu. The main pressure at that time was from the northwest down the Taejon-Taegu road. But a new menace was developing with frightening rapidity way to the southwest. For the Reds, making a huge arc around our outnumbered troops, were sending spearheads to the south coast of Korea hundreds of miles to our rear. They hoped to strike along the coast at Pusan, the vital port through which most of our supplies funneled.

It was at this time that General Walker issued his famous "stand or die" order. The 1st Cavalry and 25th Division were freshly arrived. Like the 24th Division before them, the new outfits had to learn for themselves how to cope with this Indian-style warfare for which they were so unprepared. Their soldiers were not yet battle-toughened. Taking into account the overwhelming odds, some front-line generals worried about the performance of their men and told us so privately.

General Walker put his worries on the record and at the same time issued his "no retreat" order. In a visit to the 25th Division front at Sangju in the north, he told assembled headquarters and field officers, "I am tired of hearing about lines being straightened. There will be no more retreating. Reinforcements are coming, but our soldiers have to be impressed that they must stand or die. If they fall back they will be responsible for the lives of hundreds of Americans. A Dunkerque in Korea would be a terrible blow from which it would be hard to recover."

Immediately General Walker, in a massive straightening operation of his own, took the entire 25th Division out of the line there north of Taegu. He sent them barreling to the southwest front to bear the brunt of the enemy's attempt to break through to Pusan. The operation was skillfully done and the reshuffled troops arrived just in time.

To fill the gap vacated by the 25th Division, the 1st Cavalry and the South Koreans were pulled back in a tightening operation in which we relinquished about fifty miles, but we attained a smaller, better-integrated defense arc.

It is certainly a tribute to General Walker that in the period when he had so few troops on hand and no reserves at all he was able to juggle his forces geographically so as to hold that great semicircle from the coast down the Naktong River valley to Masan on the southern coast.

I reached the southwest front in time for the 25th's first big battle after the "stand or die" order. By luck, I happened to be the only daily newspaperman on the scene. The rest of the correspondents were at Pusan covering the debarkation of the United States Marines. My colleague on the *Herald Tribune* had selected the marine landing for his own. So I left Pusan and hitchhiked my way west.

At Masan, I borrowed a jeep from the 724th Ordnance and drove in the dusk over the beautiful mountains that wind west and overlook the deep blue waters of Masan Bay. The jewel-bright rice paddies in the long, steep-sided valley held a soft sheen and the war seemed far away. But only a few nights later the sharp blue and orange tracer bullets were flicking across the valley's mouth until dawn.

The valley leads to Chindongni, where the 27th (Wolfhound) Infantry Regiment had established its headquarters in a battered schoolhouse under the brow of a high hill. Windows of the schoolhouse were jagged fragments, and glass powdered the floor. For our big 155-millimeter artillery guns were emplaced in the schoolhouse yard, and each blast shivered the frail wooden building and its windows. The terrific effect of these guns is rivaled only by the infernal explosions of aerial rockets and napalm bombs, which seem to make the sky quake and shudder.

I had been looking forward with great interest to seeing the 27th in action. Other correspondents had praised both the regiment's commander, Colonel John ("Mike") Michaelis, Eisenhower's onetime aide, and the professional hard-fighting spirit of his officers and men.

The spirit of the 27th impressed me most in the anxious "bowling-alley" days when the regiment fended off platoon after platoon of Soviet Red tanks bowled at them in the valley north of Taegu. I will never forget the message that bleated through on a walkie-talkie radio to the regiment from Major Murch's hard-pressed forward battalion. Sent close to midnight, the message said: "Five tanks within our position. Situation vague. No sweat. We are holding."

On that first night at Chindongni, I found Colonel Michaelis in a state of tension. Mike Michaelis is a high-strung, good-looking officer with much of the cockiness of an ex-paratrooper. His ambition and drive have not yet been broken by the army system.

He has inherited from his onetime boss, "Ike"—or perhaps he just had it naturally—the key to the art of good public relations: complete honesty, even about his mistakes.

That night Mike Michaelis felt he had made a bad one. His very presence in Chindongni was technically against orders. He had turned his troops around and rushed them away from assigned positions when he heard the Reds had seized the road junction pointing along the southern coast straight at Masan and Pusan. There was nothing in their path to stop them. But, reaching Chindongni, his patrols could find no enemy. There were only swarms of refugees pumping down the road. And at the very point Michaelis had left, heavy enemy attacks were reported.

Miserably, Michaelis had told his officers: "I gambled and lost. I brought you to the wrong place."

But depression could not subdue him for long. He decided he would find the enemy by attacking in battalion strength. If the road really was empty, his men might recapture the critical road junction some twenty miles to the east.

Michaelis asked the 35th Regiment to the north to send a spearhead to link up with his troops approaching the junction on the coastal route, and ordered Colonel Gilbert Check to push forward the twenty miles. The advance turned into the first major counterattack of the Korean campaign.

Michaelis told me about it in the lamplit headquarters room where conversation was punctuated by roars from the 155 guns. Again he was unhappily belaboring himself for having made a bad gamble.

It appeared that the Reds had been on the coastal road after all. Disguised in the broad white hats and white linen garb of the Korean farmer, they had filtered unhindered in the refugee surge toward Chindongni. Then, singly or in small groups, they had streamed to collecting points in the hills, some to change into uniform and others simply to get weapons.

From their mountainous hiding places they had watched Colonel Check's battalion plunge down the road. Then they had struck from the rear. Mortars and machine guns were brought down to ridges dominating the road. This screen of fire—sometimes called a roadblock—cut the road at half a dozen points between Michaelis's headquarters and Colonel Check's attacking battalion. Rescue engineer combat teams had battered all day at the hills and roads to sweep them clean of enemy, but had failed. The worst had seemingly happened. The regiment was split in two; the line of supply cut. The 35th Regiment to the north had been unable to fight its way to the road junction.

The fate of Colonel Check's battalion showed that the enemy was here in force and proved that Michaelis had been right to wheel his forces south to block this vital pathway to Pusan. But he felt he had bungled in ordering the battalion to advance so far.

"I overcommitted myself," Michaelis said miserably. "Now Check's men are stranded eighteen miles deep in enemy territory. From early reports, they've got a lot of wounded. But we've lost all contact. I sent a liaison plane to drop them a message to beat their way back here. I'm afraid we've lost the tanks."

Colonel Check's tanks took a pummeling, all right, from enemy antitank guns. But the tanks got back. Colonel Check himself told us the remarkable story as his weary battalion funneled into Chindongni at one o'clock in the morning.

"Antitank guns caught us on a curve several miles short of our objective," Check said. "Troops riding on the tanks yelled when they saw the flash, but they were too late. The tanks caught partially afire and the crews were wounded. But three of the tanks were still operable. I was damned if I was going to let several hundred thousand dollars' worth of American equipment sit back there on the road. I yelled, 'Who around here thinks he can drive a tank?' A couple of ex-bulldozer operators and an ex-mason volunteered. They got about three minutes' checking out and off they went."

One of the ex-bulldozer operators was Private Ray Roberts. His partly disabled tank led Check's column through ambush after ambush back to safety. Men were piled all over the tanks, and the gunners—also volunteers—had plenty of practice shooting back at Reds harassing them from ridges. Once the tank-led column was halted by a washout in the road. Another time Colonel Check ordered a halt of the whole column so that a medic could administer plasma.

"It might have been a damn-fool thing to do," Colonel Check said, "and the kids at the back of the column kept yelling they were under fire and to hurry up. But—well, we had some good men killed today. I didn't want to lose any more."

That night I found ex-bulldozer operator Roberts in the darkness still sitting on the tank. He was very pleased to show me every dent and hole in it. But he dismissed his feat with, "I fiddled around with the tank a few minutes. It's really easier to drive than a bulldozer. You just feel sort of funny lookin' in that darn periscope all the time."

I was amused after the roadside interview when Roberts and several of the other volunteers came up and said, "Ma'am, if you happen to think of it, you might tell the colonel that we're hoping he won't take that tank away from us. We're plannin' to git ordnance to help us fix it up in the mornin'." Private Roberts and company graduated from dogfeet to tankmen that night, but no special pleas were necessary. There were no other replacements for the wounded crews.

The battalion at final count had lost thirty men. In their biggest scrap, just two miles short of the road junction, the battalion artillery had killed two hundred and fifty enemy soldiers.

"We counted them when we fought our way up to the high ground where they had been dug in," Colonel Check said. "And earlier we caught a whole platoon napping by the roadside. We killed them all."

As Check concluded, Michaelis, with a mock grimace on his face, sent for his duffel bag, reached deep into it, and produced a bottle of scotch whisky, probably the only bona fide hard liquor in southwest Korea at the time.

"Here, you old bum," he said. "Well done."

When Check had gone, Michaelis turned to Harold Martin of the *Saturday Evening Post* and myself. We had been scribbling steadily as the colonel told of the breakout from the trap.

"Well, is it a story?" Michaelis asked. "You've seen how it is. You've seen how an officer has to make a decision on the spur of the moment and without knowing whether it's right or wrong. You've seen how something that looks wrong at first proves to be right. F'rinstance, coming down here against orders. And you've seen how a decision that seems right proves to be wrong—like sending Check's column up that road without knowing for sure what it would face. And then you've seen how a bunch of men with skill and brains and guts, like Check and the kids who drove the tanks, can turn a wrong decision into a right one. But is it a story?"

I said it was a honey and that I'd head back to Pusan first thing the next morning to file it.

With an entire battalion swarming in and around the schoolhouse, regimental headquarters was in an uproar. Colonel Michaelis had been planning to move his command post farther forward. But due to the lateness of the hour and the exhaustion of the headquarters staff and the troops, he postponed the transfer.

It was another of those chance decisions on which victories are sometimes balanced. We found out the next morning how close we had shaved our luck—again.

Half a dozen regimental staff officers, myself, and Martin were finishing a comparatively de luxe breakfast in the schoolhouse (powdered eggs and hot coffee) when suddenly bullets exploded from all directions. They crackled through the windows, splintered through the flimsy walls. A machine-gun burst slammed the coffeepot off the table. A grenade exploded on the wooden grill on which I had been sleeping, and another grenade sent fragments flying off the roof.

"Where is the little beauty who threw that?" muttered Captain William Hawkes, an intelligence officer, as he grabbed at his bleeding right hand, torn by a grenade splinter.

We tried to race down the hall, but we had to hit the floor fast and stay there. We were all bewildered and caught utterly by surprise. It was impossible to judge what to do. Bullets were spattering at us from the hill rising directly behind us and from the courtyard on the other side.

Thoughts tumbled jerkily through my mind . . . "This can't be enemy fire . . . we're miles behind the front lines . . . that grenade must have been thrown from fifteen or twenty yards . . . how could they possibly get that close . . . My God, if they are that close, they are right behind the schoolhouse . . . they can be through those windows and on top of us in a matter of seconds . . . dammit, nobody in here even has a carbine . . . well, it would be too late anyway . . . why did I ever get myself into this . . . I don't understand the fire coming from the

courtyard . . . what has happened to our perimeter defense . . . could it possibly be that some trigger-happy
GI started all this . . ."

There was soon no doubt, however, that it was enemy
fire. We were surrounded. During the night the Reds had
sneaked past our front lines, avoiding the main roads and
traveling through the mountain trails in the undefended
gap between us and the 35th Regiment to the north. In
camouflaged uniforms, they crept onto the hillside behind
the schoolhouse, while others, circling around, set up
machine guns in a rice paddy on the other side of the
schoolyard. This accounted for the vicious cross fire.

They had managed to infiltrate our defenses for several reasons. The GIs forming the perimeter defense were
utterly exhausted from their eighteen-mile foray into
enemy territory and some of the guards fell asleep. And
at least one column of the enemy was mistaken, by those
officers awake and on duty, as South Korean Police.

We had been warned the night before that South Koreans were helping us guard our exposed right flank. This
was only one of the hundreds of cases in which confusion
in identifying the enemy lost us lives. It is, of course, part
of the difficulty of being involved in a civil war.

The Communist attack against the sleeping GIs
wounded many before they could even reach for their
weapons.

I learned all of this, of course, much later. On the
schoolhouse floor, with our noses scraping the dust, the
only thought was how to get out of the bullet-riddled

building without getting killed in the process. A whimpering noise distracted my attention. In the opposite corner of the room I saw the three scrawny, dirty North Koreans who had been taken prisoner the night before. They began to crawl about aimlessly on their stomachs. They made strange moaning sounds like injured puppies. One pulled the blindfold from his eyes. On his hands and knees he inched toward the door. But the fire was too thick. The bullets of his Communist comrades cut off escape. When next I saw the three of them they were dead, lying in an oozing pool of their own blood that trickled out the room and down the hall.

The bullets cutting through the cardboard-thin walls ripped the floor boards around us, and we all kept wondering why one of us didn't get hit.

I mumbled to Harold that it looked as if we would have a very intimate blow-by-blow account of battle to convey to the American public. But he didn't hear me because one of the officers suddenly said, "I'm getting out of here," and dove out the window into the courtyard in the direction away from the hill. We all leaped after him and found a stone wall which at least protected us from the rain of fire from the high ground.

In the courtyard we found a melee of officers and noncoms attempting to dodge the incoming fire and at the same time trying to find their men and produce some order out of the chaos. Some of the soldiers in the courtyard, in their confusion, were firing, without aiming, dangerously close to the GIs racing in retreat down the hill.

Many of them were shoeless, but others came rushing by with rifles in one hand and boots held determinedly in the other.

Michaelis, his executive officer, Colonel Farthing, and company commanders were booting reluctant GIs out from under jeeps and trucks and telling them to get the hell to their units up the hill.

A ruckus of yelling was raised in the opposite corner of the courtyard. I poked my head around in time to see an officer taking careful aim at one of our own machine gunners. He winged him. It was a good shot, and an unfortunate necessity. The machine gunner had gone berserk in the terror of the surprise attack and had started raking our own vehicles and troops with machine-gun fire.

By now the regimental phones had been pulled out of the town schoolhouse and were located between the stone wall and the radio truck. Division called, and the general himself was on the phone. I heard Colonel Farthing excusing himself for not being able to hear too well. "It's a little noisy," he told the general.

Almost immediately Lieutenant Carter Clarke of the reconnaissance platoon rushed up to report he had spotted a new group of enemy massing for attack in a gulch to the north. Another officer came up with the gloomy information that several hundred Koreans had landed on the coast a thousand yards beyond.

I started to say something to Martin as he crouched by the telephone methodically recording the battle in his notebook. My teeth were chattering uncontrollably, I discovered, and in shame I broke off after the first disgraceful squeak of words.

Then suddenly, for the first time in the war, I experienced the cold, awful certainty that there was no escape. My reactions were trite. As with most people who suddenly accept death as inevitable and imminent, I was simply filled with surprise that this was finally going to happen to me. Then, as the conviction grew, I became hard inside and comparatively calm. I ceased worrying. Physically the result was that my teeth stopped chattering and my hands ceased shaking. This was a relief, as I would have been acutely embarrassed had any one caught me in that state.

Fortunately, by the time Michaelis came around the corner and said, "How you doin', kid?" I was able to answer in a respectably self-contained tone of voice, "Just fine, sir."

A few minutes later Michaelis, ignoring the bullets, wheeled suddenly into the middle of the courtyard. He yelled for a cease-fire.

"Let's get organized and find out what we're shooting at," he shouted.

Gradually the fluid scramble in the courtyard jelled into a pattern of resistance. Two heavy-machine-gun squads crept up to the hill under cover of protecting rifle fire and fixed aim on the enemy trying to swarm down. Platoons and then companies followed. Light mortars were dragged up. The huge artillery guns lowered and fired point-blank at targets only a few hundred yards away.

Finally a reconnaissance officer came to the improvised command post and reported that the soldiers landing on the coast were not a new enemy force to overwhelm us, but South Korean allies. On the hill, soldiers were silencing some of the enemy fire. It was now seven forty-five. It did not seem possible that so much could have happened since the enemy had struck three quarters of an hour before.

As the intensity of fire slackened slightly, soldiers started bringing in the wounded from the hills, carrying them on their backs. I walked over to the aid station. The mortars had been set up right next to the medic's end of the schoolhouse. The guns provided a nerve-racking accompaniment for the doctors and first-aid men as they ministered to the wounded. Bullets were still striking this end of the building, and both doctors and wounded had to keep low to avoid being hit. Because of the sudden rush of casualties, all hands were frantically busy.

One medic was running short of plasma but did not dare leave his patients long enough to try to round up some more. I offered to administer the remaining plasma and passed about an hour there, helping out as best I could.

My most vivid memory of the hour is Captain Logan Weston limping into the station with a wound in his leg. He was patched up and promptly turned around and headed for the hills again. Half an hour later he was back with bullets in his shoulder and chest. Sitting on the floor smoking a cigarette, the captain calmly remarked, "I guess I'd better get a shot of morphine now. These last two are beginning to hurt."

ACME

Deep in thought.

Marguerite Higgins with Colonel "Mike" Michaelis.

MYDANS

Four Russian-made tanks left in the wake of the 24th Infantry Division.

Tank moving up near Masan.

MYDANS

Negro infantrymen take cover in a rice paddy.

In describing the sudden rush of casualties to my newspaper, I mentioned that "one correspondent learned to administer blood plasma." When Michaelis saw the story he took exception, saying that it was an understatement. Subsequently the colonel wrote a letter to my editors praising my activities in a fashion that, I'm afraid, overstated the case as much as I perhaps originally understated it. But that Mike Michaelis should take time out from a war to write that letter was deeply moving to me. I treasure that letter beyond anything that has happened to me in Korea or anywhere. And, wittingly or unwittingly, Michaelis did me a big favor. After the publication of that letter it was hard for headquarters generals to label me a nuisance and use the "nuisance" argument as an excuse for restricting my activities.

It was at the aid station that I realized we were going to win after all. Injured after injured came in with reports that the gooks were "being murdered" and that they were falling back. There was a brief lull in the fighting. Then the enemy, strengthened with fresh reinforcements, struck again. But Michaelis was ready for them this time. At one-thirty in the afternoon, when the last onslaught had been repulsed, more than six hundred dead North Koreans were counted littering the hills behind the schoolhouse.

We really had been lucky. The enemy had attacked the first time thinking to find only an artillery unit. We had been saved by Michaelis's last-minute decision of the night before to postpone the transfer of the command post and bed down Colonel Check's battle-weary battalion at the schoolhouse. Without the presence of these extra thousand men, the Reds would easily have slaughtered the artillerymen, repeating a highly successful guerilla tactic.

The North Koreans didn't go in much for counter-battery fire. They preferred to sneak through the lines and bayonet the artillerymen in the back.

Michaelis's self-doubts were not echoed by his bosses. The series of decisions—some of them seemingly wrong at the time—that led to the battle of the schoolhouse resulted in a spectacular victory for the 27th Regiment. For Michaelis it meant a battlefield promotion to full colonel, and for Colonel Check a silver star "for conspicuous gallantry."

After the schoolhouse battle I usually took a carbine along in our jeep. Keyes, an ex-marine, instructed me in its use. I'm a lousy shot, but I know I duck when bullets start flying my way, even if they are considerably off course. I reasoned that the enemy had the same reaction and that my bullets, however wild, might at least scare him into keeping his head down or might throw his aim off. Since Keyes usually drove our jeep, I, by default, had to "ride shotgun."

Most correspondents carried arms of some kind. The enemy had no qualms about shooting unarmed civilians. And the fighting line was so fluid that no place near the front lines was safe from sudden enemy attack.

In those days the main difference between a newsman

and a soldier in Korea was that the soldier in combat had to get out of his hole and go after the enemy, whereas the correspondent had the privilege of keeping his head down. It was commonplace for correspondents to be at company and platoon level, and many of us frequently went out on patrol. We felt it was the only honest way of covering the war. The large number of correspondents killed or captured in Korea is testimony of the dangers to which scores willingly subjected themselves.

Fred Sparks of the Chicago *Daily News*, pondering about the vulnerability of correspondents, once observed: "I was lying there in my foxhole one day after a battle in which the regimental command post itself had been overrun. I started thinking to myself, 'Suppose a Gook suddenly jumps into this foxhole. What do I do then? Say to him, "Chicago *Daily News*"!'" After that Sparks announced he, too, was going to tote "an instrument of defense."

At Chindongni, when the battle was finally over, I went up to Michaelis and asked if he had any message for the division commander.

"Tell him," said Mike, "that we will damn well hold."

And they did, in this and in many subsequent battles. So did the Marines, who replaced the 27th in that area, and the 5th Regimental Combat Team, who came after the Marines. Thousands of Americans "stood and died" to hold Chindongni and the emerald valley behind it.

In battles of varying intensity, the "stand or die" order was carried out all along the Taegu perimeter. The defense arc was ominously dented on many occasions, with the most critical period being the Red offensive early in September. But it never broke. And because the line held despite the great numbers of the enemy, the fabulous amphibious landing at Inchon was made possible.

CHAPTER **9**

THE GREAT GAMBLE AT INCHON

General MacArthur says that he decided on an amphibious assault in Korea almost immediately after he learned of President Truman's decision to commit American ground troops.

"In war," the general said, "as in a card game, one tries to lead from strength. United Nations strength lay in its sea and air power." He figured that an end run, in which a substantial force would strike at the enemy rear and cut off reinforcements, was the only way to lick the numerically superior foe.

Plans for a landing began five days after the United Nations entered the war. MacArthur chose Inchon Harbor for two reasons. His advisers told him that a landing at Inchon was virtually impossible because of the unusual tides. These tides, rushing into the narrow channels,

cause the depth of the water to vary as much as thirty
feet. Then for hours each day most of the harbor becomes
a sea of mud flats. The general decided that if his advisers
felt the Inchon landing to be so difficult, the enemy probably felt the same way and could be surprised. Secondly,
our intelligence reported that the harbor was very lightly
defended.

As far as correspondents are concerned, the Inchon
landing will be remembered for a long time as one of the
biggest snafus in public-relations history. Around the
Tokyo Press Club the landing was dubbed "Operation
Common Knowledge" for many weeks in advance. But
despite this common knowledge the officers in charge
agreed that the press was in no way to be consulted about
coverage requirements. The result was that magazine
writers and columnists rode in on the first assault waves
and many first-rate daily newsmen with urgent deadlines
arrived about three days late.

My request to go aboard an assault transport was
greeted with about the same degree of horror as might
have met a leper's request to share a bunk with the admiral. Navy tradition, I was told, was strictly anti-female,
and of course there were no "facilities." (I later noted
with some glee that the flagship *McKinley* was fully
equipped with a special ladies' room.)

I gave Captain Duffy all my usual arguments: that
women war correspondents were here to stay and the
Navy might as well get used to them; that there were far
more "facilities" on a ship than in the foxholes I'd been

occupying; that it was not fair to deprive the New York *Herald Tribune* of coverage because I was a female. I might as well have been talking to myself. I was relegated to a hospital ship and told that I might not even be allowed to get off once the hospital ship reached the assault area. The prospect of wasting seven days on a ship and then not being certain of getting a story was discouraging to say the least.

But when I went to pick up my orders, Captain Duffy, apparently in a fit of absent-mindedness, handed me four neatly mimeographed sheets which announced that Miss Higgins could board "any navy ship." By the time I had grasped this wonderful switch, Captain Duffy was unavailable.

I now learned that some of the assault transports were leaving from Pusan Harbor in South Korea, and I decided to go there by air. It was an agonizing race, for I believed the transports were set to go momentarily, and even if I got there in time I wasn't at all certain of getting on one. Once in Pusan, I hitched my way to the docks. They were really roaring, with loaded trucks, tanks, amtracs, and ducks barreling past lines of troops. Almost immediately I spotted some of the male correspondents on the deck of a transport. I envied their male security from the bottom of my heart.

My first request for space was promptly refused, on the grounds that the ship was already overcrowded. I offered to sleep on deck, but it was no use. I decided to try Captain Fradd of the *Henrico*, the command ship of this par-

ticular group of transports. I was both downhearted and
tense by the time I knocked on Captain Fradd's cabin
door. But I presented my orders and stressed the fact
that I'd be happy to put my sleeping bag in the hall if
necessary.

Captain Fradd studied the orders methodically and
then said, "These look okay. I'll be happy to have you
aboard, and we happen to have a spare room—a sort of
emergency cabin."

I trembled with elation as I stammered my thanks,
and rushed away to get my gear. The transports were
due to leave in a matter of hours—there was a typhoon
threatening which would smash the ships badly if it
caught them in the harbor. I was delighted to leave so
quickly, since it meant that I would soon be completely
out of officialdom's reach. I went straight to my cabin
and locked myself in. Then I lay on the bunk with my
heart racing at every approaching sound that might mean
someone was coming to throw me out. At one o'clock
the dreaded rap came and I opened the door about three
inches.

"Ma'am," said a neat Filipino boy, "the captain wants to
know if you'd like some lunch."

From then on everything went along splendidly. The
5th Marines and the Navy weathered the horrors of having a woman around with a nonchalance that would have
annoyed Captain Duffy no end.

It took us four days to reach Inchon. I have read much
about the rigors of life on a troop transport and was pre-

pared to be uncomfortable. But I was agreeably surprised. Perhaps it was just the comparison of four months
of sleeping on the ground or in various flea-bitten huts,
but life on the *Henrico* seemed to me very pleasant for
everybody. I ate many times with the enlisted men and
enjoyed the food. It was very much of a mass-production
job, efficiently managed. You took your tray, cafeteria
style, filed past the servers, and ate standing up. The food
was warm and filling, and some of it was fresh. To my
taste it ranked one hundred per cent better than the rich,
fatty tins of C rations that were our normal fare at the
front.

During the trip Captain Fradd and Colonel Murray
briefed us fully on the technical difficulties of the battle
ahead. Our assault was to be made on "Red Beach," which
really wasn't a beach at all, but a rough sea wall of big
boulders. (The marines were definitely not looking forward with pleasure to the prospect of smashing their light
landing craft onto the stones.) At the moment of the first
landing, the wall would tower twelve feet above the water
line. Engineers had improvised wooden ladders with big
steel hooks on top to enable the first wave of troops to
scramble over the wall. Aerial photographs showed deep
trenches dug on the inland side of the wall. If any enemy
guard was still on the wall when we struck, it would be
murder. The channel approaching Inchon Harbor was so
narrow that the transports would have to anchor at least
nine miles away from the assault beaches. Space in the
harbor was reserved for warships.

A total of two hundred and sixty ships was involved in the Inchon landing. Our transports had been preceded by sixty warships, including six cruisers and six aircraft carriers. The destroyers played a remarkable role. Six of them deliberately approached within range of the shore batteries in order to draw fire. The idea was to trick the main Red defense guns into giving away their positions so that the planes and big warships could go to work on them. The trick was successful, and the destroyers were only slightly damaged. For forty-eight hours big naval guns had been pounding the shore, softening it up for the assault.

There were to be three landings in all. At dawn the first troops would storm Wolmi, a tree-covered island jutting into Inchon Bay and connected to the mainland by a long concrete causeway.

Then at five-thirty in the afternoon new marine assaults would be hurled against Red Beach, the very heart of the city of Inchon, and at Blue Beach, a long stretch of sea wall south of the city.

In between Red and Blue beaches lay the all-important tidal basin. It was the only part of the harbor that did not periodically turn into mud flats at low tide. Successful assaults on Red and Blue beaches would give us the tidal basin, where small and medium-sized craft could bring in cargo from the transports standing down the channel.

The 5th Marines were to seize the high ground just back of Red Beach and push on to the city's eastern outskirts if possible. Specially trained South Korean marines would be charged with mopping up any enemy by-passed by our troops.

At breakfast time on D day the first reports came over our radio.

"Wolmi has been secured," the radio squawked. "Casualties light."

Word spread quickly around the ship, and the normally cocky marines became even cockier. Colonel Newton, commander of the 1st Battalion, expressed the general feeling when he said immediately, "It looks as though we're in."

At three o'clock orders went out to lower the rectangular, flat-bottomed craft into the sea, and the squeaks of turning winches filled the air. From the deck I watched the same operation on the other transports, strung out down the channel as far as the eye could travel.

I was to go in the fifth wave to hit Red Beach. In our craft would be a mortar outfit, some riflemen, a photographer, John Davies of the Newark *Daily News,* and Lionel Crane of the London *Daily Express.*

There was a final briefing emphasizing the split-second timing that was so vital. The tide would be at the right height for only four hours. We would strike at five-thirty, half an hour before dead high. Assault waves, consisting of six landing craft lined up abreast, would hit the beach at two-minute intervals. This part of the operation had to be completed within an hour in order to permit the approach of larger landing ship tanks (LSTs), which would supply us with all our heavy equipment. The LSTs would hit the beach at high tide and then, as the waters ebbed away, be stranded helplessly on the mud flats. After eight o'clock, sea approaches to the assaulting marines would be cut off until the next high tide. It was a risk that had to be taken.

"Wave Number Five," someone shouted, and we threaded our way through the confusion on deck to our prearranged position. Our wave commander, Lieutenant R. J. Shening, yelled at us to be careful climbing down the cargo nets into our craft. The cargo nets were made of huge, rough ropes. The trick was to hang onto the big knots with all your strength while you groped with your feet for the swaying rungs below.

I dropped last into the boat, which was now packed with thirty-eight heavily laden marines, ponchos on their backs and rifles on their shoulders. As we shoved away from the transport sheets of spray were flung back upon us by the wind.

We must have circled almost an hour, picking up the rest of the craft in Wave Number Five. I was thoroughly keyed up, but the marines around me were elaborately calm. Two of them played gin rummy on the wooden cover over the engine. They only stopped when the lurching of the boat scattered their cards all over the wet planks.

Finally we pulled out of the circle and started toward the assault control ship, nine miles down the channel. It was an ear-shattering experience. We had to thread our way past the carriers and cruisers that were booming away at the beach, giving it a final deadly pounding. The quake and roar of the rocket ships was almost unendurable.

After twenty minutes we rounded Wolmi Island—it looked as if a giant forest fire had just swept over it. Beyond was Red Beach. As we strained to see it more clearly, a rocket hit a round oil tower and big, ugly smoke rings billowed up. The dockside buildings were brilliant with flames. Through the haze it looked as though the whole city was burning.

Red Beach stretched out flatly directly behind the sea wall. Then after several hundred yards it rose sharply to form a cliff on the left side of the beach. Behind the cliff was a cemetery, one of our principal objectives.

At the control ship we circled again, waiting for H hour. Suddenly the great naval barrage lifted and there was gigantic silence. Then the sky began to roar and the planes zoomed in, bombing and strafing the sea wall. It didn't seem possible that anything could survive the terrific hail of explosives.

Silence again. Then H hour. The first wave pulled out of the circle and headed for the beach. There were only a few more minutes to wait. We all stared fixedly at the shore—about two thousand yards away—and tried to guess, from the expressions on the faces of the seamen returning from the beach in their empty boats, what it had been like.

The control ship signaled that it was our turn.

"Here we go—keep your heads down," shouted Lieutenant Shening.

As we rushed toward the sea wall an amber-colored star

shell burst above the beach. It meant that our first objective, the cemetery, had been taken. But before we could even begin to relax, brightly colored tracer bullets cut across our bow and across the open top of our boat. I heard the authoritative rattle of machine guns. Somehow the enemy had survived the terrible pounding they'd been getting. No matter what had happened to the first four waves, the Reds had sighted us and their aim was excellent. We all hunched deep into the boat.

"Look at their faces now," John Davies whispered to me. The faces of the men in our boat, including the gin-rummy players, were contorted with fear.

Then our boat smashed hard into a dip in the sea wall. With the deadly crisscross of bullets whining above them, the marines involuntarily continued to crouch low in the boat.

"Come on, you big, brave marines—let's get the hell out of here," yelled Lieutenant Shening, emphasizing his words with good, hard shoves.

The first marines were now clambering out of the bow of the boat. The photographer announced that he had had enough and was going straight back to the transport with the boat. For a second I was tempted to go with him. Then a new burst of fire made me decide to get out of the boat fast. I maneuvered my typewriter into a position where I could reach it once I had dropped over the side. I got a footing on the steel ledge on the side of the boat and pushed myself over. I landed in about three feet of water in the dip of the sea wall.

A warning burst, probably a grenade, forced us all down, and we snaked along on our stomachs over the boulders to a sort of curve below the top of the dip. It gave us a cover of sorts from the tracer bullets, and we three newsmen and most of the marines flattened out and waited there. As we waited, wave after wave of marines hit the beach, and soon there must have been sixty or more of us lying on our bellies in the small dip.

One marine ventured over the ridge, but he jumped back so hurriedly that he stamped one foot hard onto my bottom. This fortunately has considerable padding, but it did hurt, and I'm afraid I said somewhat snappishly, "Hey, it isn't as frantic as all that." He removed his foot hastily and apologized in a tone that indicated his amazement that he had been walking on a woman. I think he was the only marine who recognized me as a woman—my helmet and overcoat were good camouflage.

The sun began to set as we lay there. The yellow glow that it cast over the green-clad marines produced a technicolor splendor that Hollywood could not have matched. In fact, the strange sunset, combined with the crimson haze of the flaming docks, was so spectacular that a movie audience would have considered it overdone.

Suddenly there was a great surge of water. A huge LST was bearing down on us, its plank door halfway down. A few more feet and we would be smashed. Everyone started shouting and, tracer bullets or no, we got out of there. Two marines in the back were caught and their feet badly crushed before they could be yanked to safety.

Davies, Crane, and I vaulted the trenches on the other side of the sea wall and ran some twenty yards across the beach. There we found a mound, only about fifteen feet high, but it gave us some protection from the bullets. In the half-dark, marines started zigzagging toward the cliff on our left, and we had an anguished view of a half dozen of them hurled to the ground by tracer bullets.

There was another terrible moment when one of the LSTs mistook some men on the top of the cliff for the enemy and began banging rockets at them. They were marines who had seized the objective only minutes before. Frantic shouts and waves from the beach finally put a stop to it, but not before a number of our men had been hit.

Six LSTs were now at the beach with their planks down. Despite the intermittent fire, they had to be unloaded. A marine colonel spotted our little group by the mound and yelled, "Hey, you big, brave marines by that mound—get the hell over here and start unloading." When we hesitated he rushed over, grabbed me by my coat lapels, and started pushing me toward the LST. I said that I'd be very glad to help if he wanted me to. When he heard my voice he dropped me hastily and very pleasantly allowed that it would undoubtedly be better if Davies, Crane, and I tended to our regular duties. I greatly admired the will and courage with which this particular marine colonel rallied his men to unload the ships in spite of severe fire.

One incident seemed to me to symbolize the technological marvel that was the Inchon landing. It started when

Crane decided to investigate the possibilities of filing our stories from an LST. He left his typewriter with us and told us sternly to stay right by the mound so that he could find us again. But only a few minutes after he left, the same marine colonel showed up and told us to get away from there. Of course we asked why.

"Because we're going to remove the mound," the colonel answered. "It's in our way."

A big bulldozer loomed up in the darkness as we edged away. A few minutes later the mound was gone and tanks, trucks, and jeeps were rolling over the spot where we had been standing. We had a terrible time locating Crane. When we finally did find him, he was so angry at what he considered our desertion that we had an even worse time convincing him that our mound just wasn't there any more.

Around seven o'clock the beach was secure and small-arms fire was insignificant. But enemy mortars were now beginning to get the range. We decided to go aboard an LST to write our stories. On our way to the wardroom we passed through a narrow alleyway which had been converted into a hospital. The doctor was operating on a wounded marine. About sixty wounded were handled by this emergency hospital that night. The number of injured was higher than at Wolmi. But, considering the natural defenses of Red Beach, we had gotten off very lightly.

As we came out of the brightly lit hospital ward the steel frame of the LST shivered. A mortar had glanced off the right side of the deck, narrowly missing some gasoline tanks stored there.

I went up to the blacked-out radio cabin to see if we could send our stories from there to the *McKinley*, the flagship of the fleet. But the radio communications had just broken down for the second time when I arrived. So we decided to try to flag a small assault boat and get back to the *McKinley* before the tide was out. We threaded our way across the beach through the heavy traffic of tanks, artillery guns, and trucks until we reached the sea wall. Even though we had been warned about the tide, it was an astonishing sight to look over the sea wall and see the boats twenty-five feet below us. We found a boat going to the *McKinley* and had to climb down a shaky ladder to get aboard.

The tide was ripping furiously when we reached the *McKinley*. It was all that our small boat could do, even with motors roaring, to hold steady against the current and give us a chance to grab the steps on the ship's side. It had started to rain, and we were drenched with rain water and spray. As I balanced precariously on the gunwale and tried to grab the steps, an officer of the deck appeared above.

"We don't want any more correspondents aboard," he shouted.

Davies and Crane and I just looked at each other. Then, without a word, we climbed on board.

The wardroom of the *McKinley* seemed the last word in warmth and luxury. They were even serving hot coffee.

The "headquarters correspondents" were putting the finishing touches on stories which they had obtained by going with MacArthur on a tour of Wolmi.

Davies and Crane were grudgingly accepted now they were on board. At least they were left alone and allowed to file their stories. I was treated like a criminal.

Captain Duffy appeared, angrily asking how I had gotten there at all. I showed him the orders that he had given me himself, and they certainly read that Miss Higgins could board "any navy ship in the pursuit of press duties."

I begged him earnestly to leave me alone long enough to write my story—a story, I couldn't help but point out, that I had gone to some effort to get. I offered to go back and sleep on the beach if he would only handle my copy without discriminating against the *Herald Tribune*. At this point one of the ship's medics made himself very unpopular with Duffy by saying that there was a completely empty room in the dispensary, complete with "facilities."

But Duffy would have none of it. He insisted on waking Admiral Doyle out of a sound sleep to deal with this Higgins menace. Once in the admiral's cabin, I tried to appease him quickly by expressing my sincere thanks for the fine treatment I had received on board the *Henrico*. And after much backing and filling it was finally agreed that I could sleep on a stretcher in the dispensary—but only for one night. Finally, around one in the morning, I was able to write the story.

After that night Admiral Doyle decreed that ladies

would be allowed on board the *McKinley* only between 9 A.M. and 9 P.M. This meant that if I got the world's most sensational scoop after nine at night, I would not be allowed aboard to write it. I felt that this put me at an unfair disadvantage with the New York *Times*, my principal competitor, and protested it fervently. As usual, my protests did no good.

From then on I slept on the docks or at the front with the troops. This was no better or no worse than what I'd grown used to in the summer war, and I didn't complain. Still, when Keyes and the rest would leave me on the docks to go out to their warm showers and real scrambled eggs, I won't pretend that I blessed the Navy. (I was much amused about a month later, when it no longer mattered, to have the Navy rule that I would be allowed aboard any ship but that I must be chaperoned at all times by a female nurse.)

The morning after the assault landing Keyes and I went ashore very early. We were worried about transportation —our own jeep was back in Pusan. Since the Army would give us no transportation officially, one of our most important jobs was scrounging. Keyes is a master at this art. Since he is an ex-marine, he is particularly good at getting what he needs from them. Actually the leathernecks are very obliging fellows anyway.

I have read President Truman's accusation that the Marines have "a propaganda machine equal to Stalin's." Actually they have almost no organized propaganda at all. I have run across only one public-relations officer attached to the Marines, and he never interfered with us in any way. This was most unusual, for I have observed that the main effect of military public-relations officers is to hamper correspondents.

The marine, as an individual, is usually extremely proud of his organization. He welcomes correspondents because they are there to tell the rest of the world about the job he is doing. Also, since they are a smaller organization than the Army, the Marines are less stuffy and less involved in red tape. It is easier for them to help you out.

This morning the shore party produced a jeep for us— or, rather, for Keyes. As we rode through the still-burning city we were astonished to find it virtually all in our hands. The civilians, afraid of being mistaken for Reds, were out in the streets by the thousands. They took elaborate care to bow and wave each time an American vehicle went by.

We located the 5th Marine command post way beyond the town. And when we finally caught up with Colonel Murray he told us, with confidence, "The beachhead? Oh, that's long been secured. Our new objectives are Kimpo airfield and Seoul."

General MacArthur's great gamble at Inchon had paid off. And in the forthcoming days I was able to fulfill the promise I had made myself—I walked back into Seoul.

It was not an easy or a pleasant walk. The United States Marines blazed a bloody path to the city. The going was particularly rough the day that Charlie Company of the 1st Marines seized a Catholic church in the center of Seoul. We did not know that the road was heavily mined until a medic jeep raced ahead of us. The jeep blew up directly in our path. Of the three people in it, only the medic survived. And his torn body and shredded, bloody face were a ghastly sight.

We quickly climbed out of our vehicles. The company commander shouted to us not to step on any freshly up-turned dirt—it might be a mine. On the rough dirt road it was difficult to follow his instructions, so we went forward gingerly on our toes.

The first platoon of Charlie Company, led by Lieutenant William Craven, stormed to the top of the bluff about three o'clock. The stinking tenements and back alleys were burning. The water front spurted mushrooms of black smoke. We had had to use white phosphorus shells and napalm fire bombs to knock out the machine guns and artillery.

"We literally had to shoot the Commies out of the church," Lieutenant Craven told us. "They were using it as a place to snipe from."

The church was a shambles. The cross had been ripped from above the altar and all religious symbols stripped from the building. Huge posters of Stalin and Kim Il Sung, the North Korean Premier, grinned down at us from the walls. There were also posters caricaturing Americans as inhuman monsters bent on murdering innocent Korean women and children. The church had obviously been used as a Communist party headquarters.

From the church we could see, in the street below, huge sandbagged barricades. The civilians told us that the bar-

ricades were mined. The Communists were using the roadblock as cover from which to shoot at us in our higher position.

The church bell hung on a wooden beam outside the
building, and we could hear the bullets clink against it.
Then suddenly we saw four Koreans standing boldly
against the sky, swinging the bell. It rang out clearly over
the racket of the battle. It was a strange, lovely sound
there in the burning city. Later on the four bell ringers
rushed up to Lieutenant Craven and said, through an interpreter, "That was for thank you."

We were giddy with victory. None of us could know
how temporary that victory was to be.

CHAPTER 10

OUR SOUTH KOREAN ALLIES

The caliber of our South Korean allies, both as soldiers and as politicians, has been almost as controversial a subject as the Korean war itself.

In the early days of the war American soldiers felt very sour about the South Korean soldiers. This was certainly understandable. In those days South Korean soldiers and officers would appropriate American army jeeps and trucks as personal property and stream southward in complete disarray. They clogged the very roads along which our soldiers were struggling north toward the front.

After the initial Red capture of Seoul on June twenty-seventh the South Korean Army of one hundred thousand men dissolved to less than twenty thousand. Many South Korean soldiers suddenly became civilians by the simple

process of changing their clothes. Others joined the refugees going south.

Many of these soldiers were reclaimed for the Army.
This was made possible through the untiring and largely
unpublicized efforts of the American officers and the men
of the Korean Military Advisory Group. Special ten-day
training systems were set up, and by the summer's end
the South Korean Army had expanded to more than one
hundred and fifty thousand. In early fall many South
Korean units were incorporated bodily into American divisions. The American officers reported enthusiastically on
their courage under fire.

From the beginning the fighting quality of the South
Koreans varied to a bewildering degree. There was great
admiration, for example, for the South Korean division
that held out on the Onjin Peninsula without help from
anybody. Other divisions turned tail and ran.

This unpredictability was hard to explain. I believe that
one explanation is that there had not been sufficient time
to build a strong officers corps. The South Korean Army,
like any other, is only as good as its officers. The Korean
Military Advisory Group (KMAG) began systematic
training of a Korean army in July of 1949. The Reds struck
eleven months later. A month before the war started Brigadier General William Roberts, head of KMAG, boasted
that the Korean GIs he had trained were good enough to
compete with the average American soldier. But he
warned that the quality of the officers was poor.

Another difficulty was that the South Koreans were

equipped largely with unwanted leftovers from the American military occupation. They had none of the essentials of modern war: tanks, adequate antitank weapons, and air power. It is true that the South Korean Army dealt successfully with most of the guerilla activity in the spring. Perhaps if they had been confronted with North Koreans who were operating alone, without foreign assistance, they might have been able to repel border attacks. But they were not even halfway prepared to fight a Russian-equipped, Russian-directed army which had been immensely strengthened by many recruits from the crack Chinese Eighth Route Army. This extraction of soldiers of Korean ethnic origin from the Chinese Eighth Route Army boosted the invading army's force to some fifteen divisions. In addition, they had more than a thousand tanks.

After the South Koreans were supplied with American equipment things improved quite a bit. The American tankmen who were attached to the Korean general's division were full of praise for the little ROK (Republic of Korea) soldiers. They told me that the South Korean engineers cleared eight miles of mined roads under heavy enemy fire and cheerfully took crazy risks to do it.

By early fall of 1950 the ten-day soldier schools were going strong. The Koreans were allowed to fire nine rounds of ammunition and were given instruction on carbines, mortars, and machine guns. But ten days is an awfully short time. Major Dan Doyle, one of the instructors, said to me, "We teach them how to dig foxholes and how to take care of their guns. But I'm afraid they have to get most of their practice in battle."

With this rushed training, it was unavoidable that the quality of some South Korean units would be low, no matter how brave they might be. It was also to be expected that the Chinese and Reds would strike hardest at the weak South Korean units. The result is that the South Koreans have been very badly hurt in this war and have frequently been unjustly blamed for failure to stand up under pressure.

One main reason for the South Koreans entering the war with an insufficient number of first-rate officers and with poor weapons was the vacillating American foreign policy. The Americans pulled the last of their occupation troops out of South Korea in midsummer of 1949. This was done in spite of vehement protests from Syngman Rhee, the President of the Republic. The Americans left because many high policy makers in Washington felt it best to write Korea off. My authority for this statement is John J. Muccio, the present Ambassador to Korea. Muccio worked hard to change the policy because he believed that the maintenance of Korea as a non-Communist bastion was as important to the morale of Asia as was Berlin's fate to the morale of western Europe.

. Militarily, America settled for half measures. We were not quite ready to go all out and announce our sponsorship of South Korea, but neither were we ready to abandon Korea completely. So we started to train a Korean army too late, and gave too little in the way of equipment.

Marines scale the breakwater that surrounds Inchon.

F4U-5 Corsairs support the marine advance.

MYDANS

The rewards of victory.

A marine sergeant interrogates two Chinese Communist prisoners.

The road back—from the Changjin reservoir, over which the
marines had to plunge fifteen miles through ice and snow and
enemy lines. They fought their way through to the coast, bringing their wounded and their equipment out with them.

The road back—marines resting by the side of their convoy.

The road back—marine casualties in an assembly area.

MYDANS

The American cemetery at Taegu.

There is no doubt that we underestimated the power and fighting ability of the Soviet-directed Oriental. But even given a lesser enemy, it was absurd to think that Korea, with its limited man power, could defend itself without tanks and planes.

I think it should be emphasized that at the time of the Red invasion South Korea was specifically excluded from General MacArthur's command. Ambassador Muccio reported directly to Washington. The responsibility for the protection of Korea lay in the inexperienced hands of the fledgling Defense Ministry, assisted by the Korean Military Advisory Group.

The confused condition of South Korea's inflationary economy was undoubtedly one reason why some Americans dismissed Korea as unsalvageable. Nevertheless, in our contradictory way, we continued to pour ECA money into the country. (Approximately $120,000,000 for the fiscal year of 1949–50.)

But when American officials began to insist that reforms be instituted in order to put some sort of lid on the wild inflation, the ECA money turned out to be a good thing. The Korean government was bluntly told that unless irresponsible government spending, money printing, and inflation in general were checked, the United States would consider withdrawing ECA assistance. Once convinced that the United States was in earnest, the legislature passed new tax laws and revenues. Since the Korean government operated all large industries, the principal source of new government income was to come from increased prices on government goods and services. There was, for example, a one-hundred-per-cent increase in rail fares and electric power.

To the amazement of many people, the economic situation improved markedly. By mid-April of 1950 prices were holding comparatively steady. Money in circulation dropped in volume and the national budget was balanced.

There is reason to believe that South Korea's increasing economic stability was one of the factors that decided the Communists to strike when they did. By Asiatic standards, South Korea had a chance of becoming an anti-Communist show place. The Reds wanted to move before South Korea became too strong. Also, our highly contradictory attitude made the Communists believe that once our occupation troops were gone we would assume no further military responsibility for South Korea. There is no doubt that United Nations intervention in Korea came as a shock to Russia and China. This has been borne out by the testimony of responsible North Korean prisoners.

As far as Korean politics went, I have often heard Asian experts in the newspaper world refer to South Korea as a police state. I had made only one visit to South Korea before the Red invasion and make no claim to being an expert on the country. But I can make something of a claim to being an expert on the police state. I spent four postwar years behind the iron curtain in Berlin and Warsaw, and also in Prague and Vienna.

There is no doubt that the three-year-old Republic of Korea, when measured by Western standards, had much to learn about making democracy work. The police had been trained by Japanese masters and were brutal in the extreme. In the general elections in 1950 there were numerous charges of police pressure, and I am sure some of them were true.

But there was no comparison between the orderly, secret balloting that I witnessed in South Korea in 1950 and the procedures used in Poland in the January 1947 voting. (This Korean election, by the way, was the first general election in Korea's four-thousand-year history.) In Poland, a bona fide police state, thousands were marched to the polls and forced to display their ballots, marked in favor of the Communist ticket. The alternative was a stint in prison or dismissal from their jobs.

In deciding whether to place a country in a police-state category, I think it is always wise to avoid black-and-white decisions. Let me put it this way. From what I have seen and read about Korea, the margin of individual freedom seemed to be increasing before the Red invasion. It was increasing much too slowly to suit most Americans, but still it was doing so. From what I have seen and read about Poland, the margin of individual freedom is rapidly diminishing. Korea had a long way to go to catch up—or down—with Poland.

The Korean Republic was established in August of 1948. This followed years of oppression by the Japanese, who had annexed the peninsula in 1910. For three years after World War II, Korea was governed by American occupation forces. Its Constitutional Assembly was chosen under the auspices of the temporary United Nations Commission. The Constitution was supposed to apply to all of Korea. But the Russians ordered the North Koreans to boycott the government sponsored by the United Nations. In September of 1948 the Reds established a regime of their own with a capital at Pyongyang.

The northern half of Korea is the larger geographically and the country's main industries are located there. But the North holds only nine million inhabitants as compared to some twenty million in South Korea. The 38th parallel of latitude, which ultimately became the demarcation line between Red Korea and Free Korea, has no basis in international law. This parallel was selected arbitrarily by the United States and Russia to help solve the problem of splitting up the Japanese war prisoners. According to the agreement, all Japanese who surrendered above the parallel would be cared for by the Soviet Union. All those who surrendered below the parallel would go into United States POW camps. When it proved impossible to establish a coalition government acceptable to both Russia and the United States, the parallel turned into a permanent barrier bristling with guns and barbed wire.

The Korean Republic had a unicameral legislature elected directly by the people. The most powerful official was the venerable President, Syngman Rhee. When I last saw him in September of 1950 he appeared the very essence of old age. He was small, slight, very wrinkled, and his voice was shaky and faded. He admitted to seventy-eight years. But, whatever his age, it had in no way blunted his will.

Rhee has frequently been called reactionary. George M. McCune, in his book, *Korea Today*, said that in the early days of 1945–46, "Many Americans objected to Rhee's reactionary methods and favored Koreans who would be more conciliatory toward the Russians." In the light of subsequent events, it is hard to hold Rhee's anti-Soviet stand against him.

I have had frequent talks with President Rhee about police activities in Korea. He has always insisted that the rule of law prevailed and that the police were not allowed to make arrests without warrants. But I happen to know that during the confusion of the Red invasion the rule of law was frequently ignored. I have seen captured Communist suspects summarily and brutally executed. Rhee insists that these incidents are the inevitable result of the passions aroused by the war and that his government did its best to control them.

Rhee seemed to me a man of autocratic temperament but sincere democratic convictions. He believed in the democratic way for the Korean people, but every so often he has taken undemocratic short cuts to achieve immediate aims. It infuriated him to be called reactionary. In the defense of his government, he pointed to the widespread land reform inaugurated in June of 1950. He also referred to government plans for the sale of former Japanese industries to small businessmen and to the government ownership of all big industry. I think he regards himself as a sort of oriental Winston Churchill. He knows both England and America well, since he has passed most of his life in exile. For many years Rhee was the head of the group of Korean patriots-in-exile who were agitating for Korean independence.

I remember Rhee's final words on that Indian-summer day in September when victory seemed so deceptively close.

"Your government must learn, as we have," he said, "that there is no compromise with the Reds. It will always be a trick for them to gain time and lull your suspicions. The next time they strike it may be, for your world, too late."

CHAPTER **11**

THE CHINESE INTERVENTION

The September successes at Inchon and Seoul broke the back of the North Korean Army. With the 10th Corps astraddle their main supply routes in the north, and the Eighth Army hammering at them from the south, the enemy disintegrated. The North Koreans needed outside help to prevent a United Nations victory. At this point the Soviet world decided that the issues of prestige and military strategy involved were worth the risk of a world conflict. On October 14, 1950, Chinese troops smashed across the Yalu River.

The possibility of Chinese intervention had been obvious from the moment President Truman sent American air power into combat. Unless we chose to abandon Korea entirely, it was a chance we had to take. But the actual timing of the Chinese intervention came as a complete surprise to high-ranking military men, including General MacArthur. They had figured that if the Chinese were going to strike, midsummer would have been the logical time. Between June and September the Chinese could easily have pushed our tiny force out of Korea at very little cost to themselves. It was hard to explain why Mao Tse-tung had waited until we had built up our fire power to a point where, even in retreat, we could take a punishing toll of lives.

The most convincing explanation seems to me to be that the Chinese stayed out of the war just as long as there was any hope that the North Koreans could lick us on their own. That hope came very close to reality until the Inchon landing suddenly changed the picture. POW intelligence indicates that sometime in late September the Chinese troops along the Manchurian border were told to get ready for combat.

Fear of Chinese intervention was one reason why General MacArthur felt so strongly that military operations in Korea should be completed in the shortest possible time. He hoped that if we could move fast enough to confront the Chinese with the *fait accompli* of a United Nations victory, they would hesitate to reopen the war. That is why he refused to postpone the Inchon landing when the American Joint Chiefs of Staff urged him to wait until October. (This temporary uncertainty about the timing of the Inchon landing is probably one reason why it was such a surprise to the Communists. One good thing about not knowing our own minds is that this prevents the Red intelligence network from knowing them either.)

Chinese influence in the Korean war was considerable from the beginning. I remember as early as July being present at a forward South Korean outpost when a Chinese-speaking prisoner of war was brought in. In his pockets were Chinese Army manuals, complete with pictures of Mao Tse-tung, the Chinese dictator, and Chu Teh, the head of the Chinese armies. We learned, upon questioning him, that he had parents in Korea, but he had spent so much time in China that he could scarcely remember his native tongue.

With the benefit of hindsight, I can recall other warnings of the extent of the Chinese involvement. At the time of the battle for Seoul we wondered why the North Koreans fought so desperately when it was seemingly useless. The battle involved house-to-house, cellar-to-cellar, roof-to-roof fighting of the most vicious sort. We had to burn down many acres of the city with artillery and flame-throwing tanks.

The day of Seoul's fall, September twenty-eighth, Keyes Beech and I paid a visit to the Chosun Hotel. We were greeted there by the assistant manager, Wang Han Sok. He was rather excited over what he considered a puzzling incident. The Communist manager, who had been sent down from Pyongyang, had absconded with all the hotel keys and records. When asked for an explanation of this apparently meaningless action, he had said, "We are coming back soon—help is coming." We thought it was just a bluff.

In early October, before the crossing of the 38th paral-

lel, Chinese Premier Chou En-lai released a statement over
the Peking Radio in which he pledged, "China will always
stand on the side of the Korean people . . . and will
support their liberation of Korea."

Despite the threat of intervention implicit in this statement, General MacArthur sent his forces into North Korea
on October eleventh. This was done with the full official
approval of the United Nations and was in pursuance of
his military mission to restore "peace and security in all
Korea."

At this point various nations secretly urged that Mac-
Arthur be told to halt, first at the 38th parallel and then
north of Pyongyang. But the United Nations itself never
withdrew its original assignment.

In official American opinion the question of stopping
at this or that parallel had no bearing on the Chinese intervention. In support of this view, various Chinese state-
ments are cited. Wu Hsiu-chuan, the Chinese Communist
delegate to the United Nations, took pains to stress that
the Chinese objected to American presence *anywhere* in
Korea. From the beginning the Chinese have labeled
American intervention even south of the 38th parallel as
aggression. The Peking Radio had pledged the liberation
of all of Asia from the non-Communists. America felt that
if the North Koreans could not push us out, the Chinese
would try to finish the job.

Both the British and Madame Pandit, Indian Ambassa-
dress to the United States, disagree with this view. They
insist that the crossing of the parallel aroused fears in Pe-

king that we would invade China proper. It was these
fears, they believe, that prompted the Chinese to intervene.

Before crossing the parallel General MacArthur broadcast two pleas to the North Koreans to surrender and accept United Nations rule for the entire country. These
offers were defiantly rejected. It seems reasonable that if
the Chinese intervention were based on security consider-
ations, they would have urged their Korean protégé to
accept the offer of United Nations rule. It would have
been a rule in which their Soviet protector would certainly have had a big say. But the United Nations rule was
turned down without hesitation.

A few Chinese were in Korea even before we crossed
the parallel. But the main body of Chinese began slipping
across the Yalu River by night on October fourteenth.
(The Yalu divides North Korea and Manchuria.) Two
weeks later they struck at forward columns of the Eighth
Army, which was approaching the Yalu in pursuit of
North Korean remnants. This forced an abrupt withdrawal
while the Eighth Army regrouped on the Chongchon
River.

General MacArthur then issued a communiqué in which
he announced that he was confronted with a totally new
war. He added that since the Reds were possibly backed
by a large concentration in the sanctuary of Manchuria,
a trap was being "surreptitiously laid calculated to encom-
pass the destruction of the United Nations Forces."

Nevertheless, nineteen days later he ordered the highly

controversial "end the war" offensive. He was accused of walking into the very trap he had just described.

The offensive, like Inchon, was a gamble. But this time we lost. There is no doubt that General MacArthur was laboring under unprecedented military handicaps. Before the offensive we had no clear idea of what forces opposed us. Field intelligence was hampered by the severest limitations. Aerial reconnaissance was impossible. The avenues of advance from the border were only a night's march and provided maximum natural concealment.

And yet the enemy capabilities—the concentration of reinforcements which MacArthur himself had described —had not changed. In order to understand why MacArthur discounted his own warning, it is necessary to review the events of the nineteen days before the offensive. During this time the Chinese yielded a lot of ground to our probing. The Peking Radio doggedly broadcast the fiction that the troops in Korea were only volunteers. At the same time the 10th Corps continued to push forward successfully on the east coast. The 17th Regiment raised the flag on the Yalu River.

As MacArthur himself has stated, he gambled that the Chinese in Korea were only token units, sent to fulfill the letter but not the spirit of their promises to help Korea. MacArthur's aides say that he also hoped that Peking would be discouraged by the devastating bombing of North Korea.

Air-force close-support capabilities were once again overestimated. MacArthur's communiqué announcing the "end the war" offensive confidently said that the "air forces have successfully interdicted the enemy's lines of supply from the north so that further reinforcement therefore has been sharply curtailed and essential supplies markedly limited."

Tokyo was apparently overly impressed by reports from prisoners of war that many Chinese were terrified of our fire power and ready to give up. Some of MacArthur's aides pictured the Chinese as seriously demoralized.

MacArthur maintains that it was far better to discover the enemy's intentions when we did rather than to wait for him to complete his build-up and strike at a time of his own choosing. His critics do not disagree in principle, but they feel that he found out the hard way. Instead of an "end the war" offensive they believe there should have been a reconnaissance in force.

MacArthur's critics also claim that, in view of the possible strength of the enemy, our forces were far too thinly scattered. In the northeast the 10th Corps troops were strung out from Wonsan on the coast to the wild mountains around the Changjin reservoir. Some Korean forces were rushing toward Siberia up a coastal road. By spreading itself so thinly in the west, the Eighth Army made it possible for the Chinese to break through anywhere.

General Walker, in a defense of the abortive offensive, stated that it had saved his army from possible destruction. But the critics say that the Eighth Army went on the move at a time when its supply lines were insecure, when it had no prepared defensive positions to fall back on, and when guerillas were attacking its rear bases.

Finally, the critics assert that MacArthur's forces were deployed in a manner suitable for fighting the remnants of the North Korean Army when the war with the Chinese had already begun.

From the psychological point of view it would certainly have been better if MacArthur had labeled his offensive a final test of Chinese intentions rather than a "general assault, which, if successful, should for all practical purposes end the war." General MacArthur has privately admitted that he made a mistake in issuing such an optimistic communiqué. He explained that his references to bringing our troops to Tokyo were intended as reassurances to the Chinese that we would get out of Korea the moment the Manchurian border was reached.

At any rate, the assault uncovered the might of two Chinese armies, more than thirty divisions. The Chinese counterattack hurled us out of North Korea in only a month.

During that period the Western World presented a frightening picture of disunity. Instead of blaming the Chinese, we hunted frantically in our own ranks for scapegoats. It almost seemed as if we were looking for someone to condemn on our own side, so that we could avoid facing the fact that China was warring against us. General MacArthur, of course, was on the griddle. The man who had been hailed as a military genius because of the Inchon landing was now accused by some American newspapers as militarily incompetent.

In the uproar that was raised against him MacArthur

was in a way a victim of his own public personality. He was caught in the trap of his own legend: that of a lofty, infallible genius. This legend has been built up assiduously by his aides, who for years have refused to admit that their leader could ever make a mistake. When MacArthur underestimated the enemy and showed his military fallibility, the world was shocked and angry. He had broken his legend, and the world could not forgive him for being human after all.

Personally, I have the highest respect and a deep sense of loyalty toward General MacArthur. I have talked with him many times, and my impression is of a man who is beyond personal ambition, whose selflessness in his country's cause is complete. I do not know nearly enough about military theory or practice to evaluate the scope of MacArthur's miscalculations, but I can report that even his severest critics do not believe that this setback in North Korea can change his over-all place in history as a great soldier.

One thing is sure. No amount of military genius could have prevented the Chinese from hurling us back a considerable distance in Korea once they chose to strike. The odds were overwhelming; in view of their man power and resources, our only possible choice was to retreat. Our military knew from the beginning that if the Chinese intervened in force, committing their best troops, we would have to start running. MacArthur's maneuver had no bearing on the ultimate outcome, which was one of the greatest strategic withdrawals in our history. A different tactic might possibly have slowed the retreat a few days, but that is all.

The retreat of the United Nations from North Korea was one of the major reversals in our history. But it was a fighting retreat and produced one of the epics of United States military history. The marine breakout from their entrapment at Yudamni is symbolic of how a military situation at its worst can inspire fighting men to perform at their best.

CHAPTER **12**

EPIC MARINE "ADVANCE TO THE REAR"

On December 4, 1950, the Peking Radio announced confidently to the world, "The annihilation of the United States 1st Marine Division is only a matter of time." The Chinese certainly had good reason for their cockiness. At the time of the great Chinese counteroffensive the leathernecks were trapped in the icy wastes of the Changjin reservoir, high in the purple mountains of northeast Korea. They were surrounded on all sides by Chinese armies and were outnumbered at least six to one.

But there was never any thought of surrender. I was present, one day after that Peking broadcast, at a briefing held in the snowy fields of Hagaru. The snow lashed hard at the raw faces of a dozen marine officers as they stood in the zero temperature listening to the words of their commander, Lieutenant Colonel Ray Murray.

"At daylight," Murray said, "we advance to the rear. Those are division orders." Then he added, almost argumentatively, "We're going to come out of this as marines, not as stragglers. We're going to bring out our wounded and our equipment. We're coming out, I tell you, as marines or not at all."

The men to whom he spoke had just fought five days and five nights to lead their men out of the icy Communist trap at Yudamni. It had been a Korean Valley Forge, and worse than anything in marine history. The men were exhausted, and the tension among them was all-pervasive. They had the dazed air of men who have accepted death and then found themselves alive after all. They talked in unfinished phrases. They would start to say something and then stop, as if the meaning was beyond any words at their command.

Despite what they had gone through, they took this withdrawal order hard. While Murray spoke I watched their faces, and their expressions were of deeply hurt pride. From Château-Thierry to Guadalcanal, from Eniwetok to Iwo Jima, marines had never fought any way but forward. Many thousands had died in those strange-sounding places, as they had here at Yudamni. But never had the marines stopped fighting until, to use the matter-of-fact language of the corps, the objective was secured.

Sensing the atmosphere, Colonel Murray went on somewhat harshly, "This is no retreat. This is an assault in another direction. There are more Chinese blocking our path to the sea than there are ahead of us. But we're going to get out of here. Any officer who doesn't think so will kindly go lame and be evacuated. I don't expect any takers."

This briefing started the last phase of the fighting retreat. The terrible trek out of the mountains cost more than Tarawa or Iwo Jima. There were nearly five thousand army and marine casualties, including dead, missing, wounded, and frostbite cases. Never brush off the word "frostbite." For many marines it meant amputated fingers, toes, feet, or legs.

As I pieced it together there on the plateau, and later at Marine division headquarters, the full story of the first marine withdrawal in history begins properly in mid-November. It was then that the 1st Marine Division began pushing north from Hamhung on the winding road leading to the Changjin reservoir.

There were warnings even then. The enemy harassed the supply lines, and the frequent ambushes showed that he was present in considerable numbers between the supply base at Hamhung and the forward troops at the reservoir. Still it was believed that there was only a division in the area, and they seemed to be yielding to our pressure.

In reality, as Private Richard Bolde so well described it, "It was a mousetrap. The Chinese would let us in but they wouldn't let us out."

On November twenty-fourth the 5th Marines were ordered to cross the snowy mountain passes and seize the oriental shanty town of Yudamni. The town is a series of rickety clapboard huts, shared, with complete impartiality, by humans and oxen with great wintry beards. Yudamni was deep on the northwestern side of the reservoir. The 7th Marine Regiment, then located at Hagaru on the southern tip of the reservoir, was to follow after the 5th. The 1st Marine Regiment was moving into Koto, about eight miles below the reservoir, at the point where the road drops off the plateau and descends sharply to the coastal plain three thousand feet below.

It is now an open secret in Korea that the marines believe that faulty generalship was partly responsible for the extent of their entrapment. The marines were a part of the 10th Corps and so were subject, for the first time in their history, to army orders. The marines now claim that they had qualms from the beginning about the army orders which sent them into Yudamni valley. According to the marines, by November twenty-fourth there were strong reports of a Chinese build-up south and west of Yudamni. That meant that the enemy was on their west flank and to their rear. These reports were borne out by the dangerously persistent attacks on the only line of supply.

Then on November twenty-fifth the great Chinese offensive slashed at the Eighth Army. The Eighth Army had been situated southwest of the marine forward spearheads. When it was hurled back, the marines were stripped of protection for their western flank. The strength of the assault on the Eighth Army left no doubt that great masses of Chinese must be swarming over the spiny mountain ridges that separated the two American forces.

Nonetheless, even after November twenty-fifth, the 10th Corps ordered the marines to keep on advancing. Although they were already under attack, they did so, but they questioned the wisdom of the move. On November twenty-sixth the 5th Marines seized Yudamni, and the next day they began attacking westward.

But in the meantime the Chinese infiltrated in back of the spearheads. They cut the road between Yudamni and Hagaru, and between Hagaru and Koto. The marines were trapped on all sides by a sea of Chinese.

In justification of the 10th Corps order to the marines to keep on attacking, I have been told that by sending the marines westward the Army hoped to strike at the Chinese rear and deflect pressure from the Eighth Army. But the marines contend that, since the strength of the enemy had been revealed, it was a mistake to extend their outnumbered forces any further. They believe they should have been ordered back to Hamhung immediately. Two regiments, they argue, could not possibly deflect the dozen or more divisions pushing south. The attack out of Yudamni was all the more ill advised, in the marines' opinion, because of the tortuous and vulnerable supply route.

In the early morning hours of November twenty-eighth the worst happened. Between six and eight Chinese divisions (estimates range from eighty thousand to one hundred and twenty thousand men) converged on the marines. The most vicious assaults hit the 5th and the 7th Marines, trapped at Yudamni with their supply lines already cut. From this time until they broke out of Yudamni, the marines had to be supplied by air. Big Air Force C-119s used gaudy red-and-yellow chutes to drop ammo and food. The chutes contrasted weirdly with the spectacular black-and-white country.

At four o'clock on the morning of November twenty-eighth the 7th and 5th Marines reported that they were "heavily engaged" and sent a plea for maximum air support. Finally, without waiting for word from Corps, Marine Division instructed the regiments to stop attacking and hold where they were. The next day the orders came to fight their way back from Yudamni to Hagaru.

"Those five days and nights fighting our way out of nightmare alley were the worst thing that ever happened to the marines," Colonel Murray told me. "The rest was nothing compared to that. (The trip from Hagaru to the coast.) Night after night near Yudamni I thought I'd never see daylight again."

Yudamni was an ideal trap; steep-sided valleys led to it along a narrow, icy road. The Chinese hugged the ridges, and the marines were easy targets. Then the temperature dropped way below zero. Guns and vehicles froze. The marines had to chip the ice off the mortars to fire them. Carbines jammed in the cold.

There was no refuge for the wounded. They had to take their chances in the convoy, under attack at every point. Murray brought out two wounded men strapped across the radiator of his jeep, their hands and legs frozen. Many wounded were on stretchers for more than seventy-two hours. Exposure and frostbite complicated their chances of survival enormously. Nothing could be done about it.

Riflemen were given the job of clearing the ridges as the convoy inched forward. They were frequently slaughtered. Whole platoons disappeared.

I had a long talk with Lieutenant John Theros, forward air observer with the 7th Marines, and I think he can describe the general setup better than I can.

"It's a hard kind of fighting to explain," he said, "except to say that everyone in the valley either came out with a Purple Heart or came within inches of getting one. Look at me. My pant leg has two bullet rips. And my canteen that I carried on my hip is an old sieve.

"I used to kid some of my friends about leading a soft, fat-cat life back at regiment. Well, at Yudamni there was no such thing as a safe place. The Chinese headed for the command posts—they liked killing colonels just as much as killing privates.

"But the guys you ought to write about are guys like Captain Hull of our battalion. He was a company commander, and what a terrific guy. He was wounded going into the valley, but he wouldn't be evacuated. Then the Chinese really let us have it, and Captain Hull's company got pushed off the hill they were holding. He only had forty-nine men left in his company, but he was mad and so were the men. They went back up that hill, and the guys said they were stomping over frozen dead gooks all the way up. But they got shoved down again, and this time Hull was reported hit. We didn't hear anything more about him at battalion.

"I thought sure he was done for then, and I remember sitting around during a lull that night saying what a terrific guy Captain Hull had been. And suddenly the old bastard walks in with two more wounds—one high up in the chest and one in the shoulder.

"That night we had been forming what we called the 'damnation battalion.' Our regiment had been so cut up that we were putting all the remnants in it—platoon leaders without platoons, mortar men without a mortar company, truck drivers without trucks—we formed them all up in the 'damnation battalion.' Well, Hull didn't have any company left to speak of, and damned if he didn't go to the major running the 'damnation battalion' and volunteer. He said to the major, 'I'm not much good at shooting in this condition, but I can still walk, and if you've got any men who want to follow me, I'll lead 'em.' He marched out of the valley with the rest of us. You know, you hear stories about comrades of battle getting to be closer than brothers. I guess it's true. I'd do anything for that Captain Hull, and I don't even know his first name."

The 7th and 5th Regiments were now operating for the first time under joint orders and without benefit of division guidance. As they battered their way along they came across Fox Company of the 7th. The company had been isolated for five days on a hilltop.

There were only seventy-five men left in Fox Com-

pany, and every one of them was wounded. But, except
for the most critical cases, they were still shooting. They
used piled-up bodies of dead Chinese to protect their
foxholes.

On December third and fourth the ten-mile-long marine caravan finally broke out of the Yudamni valley. They
reached the temporary haven of the saucer-shaped Hagaru plateau. They had cracked half a dozen roadblocks
and fixed numerous bridges under fire. Time after time
they had fought off the Chinese, who would swoop down
on them and throw phosphorus hand grenades into the
truckloads of screaming wounded.

The marines had even brought some army wounded
with them—remnants of a 7th Division unit that had been
smashed on the eastern side of the reservoir. The Chinese
had attacked the ambulances, and most of the wounded
had been spilled out onto the ice. In order to rescue them,
the marines had to dodge vicious enemy fire.

I had arrived at Hagaru as the last of the marines filtered through the pass. As our "gooney bird" DC-6 circled
over the icy humps that passed for an airstrip, our pilot
pointed to the snow-topped foxholes in the ridges. These
foxholes, which were in easy rifle range of the field, con-
stituted the limits of our defense perimeter. North, south,
east, and west there was nothing but gooks.

Between December third and sixth forty-five hundred
wounded and frostbite cases were flown out of the Hagaru strip. Doc Herring, naval surgeon attached to the 1st
Marine Division, was on hand at the strip. He had the

difficult job of deciding which men were sufficiently hurt
to justify flying them out. No one could go unless it was
absolutely necessary: every man able to shoot was needed
for the forthcoming fight. Hagaru was only twenty minutes from the coast by air. But it was sixty tortuous, pre-
cipitous walking miles. And for the first twenty miles, to
the bottom of the plateau at Chinhungni, the marines
would have to punch through a solid Chinese wall.

As I looked at the battered men there at Hagaru, I
wondered if they could possibly have the strength to
make this final punch. The men were ragged, their faces
swollen and bleeding from the sting of the icy wind.
Mittens were torn and raveled. Some were without hats,
their ears blue in the frost. A few walked to the doctor's
tent barefoot because they couldn't get their frostbitten
feet into their frozen shoepacs. They were drunk with
fatigue, and yet they were unable to shrug off the tension that had kept them going five days and nights without sleep and often without food. (It took at least an hour
to thaw out a can of frankfurters and beans, and there had
seldom been an hour to spare for such matters.)

Colonel Murray was a haggard ghost of the officer
whom I had watched lead the 5th Marines assault on Red
Beach in the happy days of the successful Inchon landing.
But his driving will was still there. When I entered the
regimental tent he was hard at work on plans for the
fight to Koto, eight miles away.

Militarily speaking, the colonel explained, the breakout
from Yudamni had been possible because the Chinese

had not observed one of the basic principles of war: they had failed to concentrate their forces where they would do the most good.

"If the Chinese had concentrated their troops at the point of exit," Murray said, "we could never have gotten out of the trap. By trying to keep us consistently encircled, they dispersed their strength."

"Do you think they'll make the same mistake again?" I asked.

Murray's answer was simple. "They've got to," he said.

And they did. The marine trek from Hagaru to Koto lasted two bloody days. But even as the spearheads of the 7th Regiment reached Koto's bleak haven, the men of the 5th were still at Hagaru fighting off a furious night attack aimed at wiping out the rear guard. With dawn and the arrival of air cover, the 5th Marines thrust back the Chinese.

An aerial curtain of marine Corsairs and navy fighters protected the head and tail of the column as it wound over the road to Koto. Only the drivers stayed in the vehicles. Everyone else walked, with weapons at the ready. When the Chinese attacked there was no time to waste scrambling out of jeeps and trucks. So the caravan crawled along, fighting off attacks from the sides and rear.

By journalistic good fortune, I was on hand in Koto to meet the marines. I had hitched a ride in a fighter-bomber piloted by Captain Alfred McCaleb, going to Koto to fly out wounded. There were only three of these planes in service that first day. One blew a tire and the other tripped over on the runway, so that left the main burden on McCaleb. I later learned that McCaleb personally flew out nearly a hundred men. It was the first time in history that fighter-bombers were used in this way.

There was an unmistakable difference in the attitude of the marines arriving in Koto and that of the haggard men I'd seen at Hagaru. The new feeling seemed to be, "If we've got this far, we're bound to make the rest."

I was deeply impressed by the large number of Korean refugees who followed after the marines and squatted stubbornly in the snowy fields. Our presence in Korea had brought destruction to their towns and death to their people. Yet here were nearly a thousand people who had left their homes and followed our troops rather than remain and face the Chinese Communists.

It was now December seventh, still very cold, but at least the racing winds were letting up. The canyon road that lay ahead was the steepest and narrowest part of the journey. But it was only ten more miles to Chinhungni, and Chinhungni was the doorway to safety.

At General Smith's tent, very popular with the marines because of its big iron stove, a new crisis had turned up. It seemed that a bridge had been blown on the mountain road ahead of us. Unless it was repaired, the marines would have to abandon all their equipment and fight their way across the mountains as scattered units. This they certainly didn't want to do. And yet it was vital to save time, since every day lost meant more Chinese between them and the sea.

MYDANS

One of the mass United Nations graves in Korea.

MYDANS

North Korean prisoners.

MYDANS

Victims.

MYDANS

Chonui, a typical Korean town.

MYDANS

Men of the 24th Infantry Division moving forward.

It looked as if they would have to pluck a new bridge from the sky. And, in a very short time, that is exactly what they did. Eight spans of a treadway bridge hurtled out of the big bellies of Air Force flying boxcars to the waiting marine engineers below. Despite the parachutes, the heavy steel spans dug deep into the ground. But they were undamaged. Plans could be made to go ahead.

The 7th Marine Regiment was to seize key ridges overlooking the canyon road between Koto and the bottom of the mountain. From the south, the first battalion of the 1st Marines would fight north toward the 7th. Task Force Dog would guard the road from Chinhungni to the coast, in an effort to make a speedy exit possible. A thick air cover was called for the next day to help the marines fight for the important ridges.

But the air cover never came. On December eighth a thick mixture of fog and snow masked Koto and the jagged peaks around it. One "gooney bird" probed miraculously through the blur, and that was all. The familiar drone of planes was strangely absent, and a glacial, primeval silence settled over the hundreds of tents dotting the Koto plain.

It was with cruel suspense that division officers waited for word from their troops who were attacking the critical ridges without benefit of air cover. The Chinese fought hard, and it was not until late in the day that the initial objectives were reported secured. Actually those ridges were never totally secure: skirmishes raged on them the entire time that the caravan rolled by on the road below.

But the skirmishes kept the Chinese busy and apparently prevented them from making a major attack on the caravan.

The next day was luckier. The fog cleared overnight, and on December ninth fleets of marine and navy fighters swooped low to protect the marine engineers as they pressed forward to build their bridge. Back at Koto, preparations were made for the final exit once the bridge was completed. Tents were dismantled, stoves piled on trucks, and time bombs set in the huge dump of ammunition that had to be left behind.

The two-motored C-47's were scooting in and out regularly, and by afternoon all the wounded were out. But there was not enough time for aerial evacuation of the dead. Three mass graves were dynamited out of the frozen earth. Then the dead were buried by the hundreds. The marines were wrapped in their ponchos. Some British commandos still wore their berets. They were laid beside men of the Army's 7th Infantry Division in a kind of final fraternity.

In the first grave there were only thirty bodies, so small wooden crosses could be put up inscribed with name, rank, and outfit. But the other two graves were marked by single red-and-white wooden poles. The graves registration officer paced off the spot and drew a map in case we should ever come back. The chaplain recited "The Lord Is My Shepherd" to a small audience of two privates, a few reporters, and several officers. But the tobogganing wind swept away his words.

Later on in the morning I was in the command post when an excited marine major burst open the flimsy wooden door to tell General Smith that the bridge was ready. We could start rolling.

I had been asked by a company of the 5th Marines, with whom I had made the landing at Inchon, to walk out with them. Of course I wanted very much to do so. But General Smith had a strong seizure of chivalry that afternoon and insisted that the walkout was too dangerous.

I walked down the mountain anyway—at least a good half the way. It was a reverse hike. Since I had to, I flew out of Koto to Hamhung. Once there, I took a weapons carrier to the bottom of the mountain. Then I hiked up the mountain for about five miles, past the streams of vehicles heading for the sea. After I had climbed far enough to get a sweeping view of the steep road and the valley below it, I headed back down. It was tough on the feet but worth every blister to be with the marine foot troops as they came at last to safety.

It was a battle all the way. The frost and wind, howling through the narrow pass, were almost as deadly as the enemy. Bumper to bumper, trucks, half-tracks, and bulldozers slipped and scraped down the mountain. Half a dozen vehicles skidded and careened off the road. Mortars lobbed in, and sometimes the convoy had to stop for hours while engineers filled in the holes. It was a struggle to keep from freezing during these waits.

Once the convoy had to stop to accept the surrender

of some Chinese soldiers. "They popped out of their holes at dawn and handed us their guns," said Major Sawyer, who led the advance guard. "It was very strange. But they were in miserable shape—maybe they had just had enough."

Most of the marines were so numb and exhausted that they didn't even bother to take cover at sporadic machine-gun and rifle fire. When someone was killed they would wearily, matter-of-factly, pick up the body and throw it in the nearest truck.

On the road the first morning, David Duncan, brilliant photographer for *Life*, was busy taking pictures. He took one of a marine patiently hacking out his breakfast from a frozen tin of beans. The beans were encased in ice crystals, and little ice crystals had also formed on the marine's beard. His eyes were running, and his cold fingers could scarcely manipulate the spoon. Thinking of his Christmas issue, Duncan asked the marine, "If I were God and could give you anything you wanted, what would you ask for?"

"Gimme tomorrow," said the marine, and went on hacking at the beans.

About twenty-five thousand marines got "tomorrow" as their Christmas present. The first elements of the convoy poured out of the shivering nightmare of the trap around two in the morning on Sunday, December tenth. It had taken them fourteen hours to go ten miles. After that, in spite of several bad ambushes, the convoys flowed in intermittently. And late that night the bulk of the marines were safely in Hamhung, warm and sleeping.

Many of the marines were at first too dazed to realize that their ordeal was actually over. But gradually a feeling of elation spread. I talked again to Lieutenant Theros, who had told me the story of Captain Hull.

"We've really got it made now," he said. "I don't know if I can tell you how the guys feel. It's not having to look for a place to hide . . . it's being able to sleep without feeling guilty . . . it's being able to eat something warm . . . it's not having to spend most of your time just trying not to freeze to death . . . maybe it doesn't sound like much."

The marines had come to Hamhung in good order, bringing their equipment, their wounded, and their newly dead, just as Colonel Murray had said they would on that cold morning in Hagaru. As they boarded the transports in Hungan Harbor, the places for which they had fought so hard—Yudamni, Hagaru, Koto, Chinhungni—were already swarming with Chinese. But as far as the reputation of the United States Marines was concerned, it did not matter. Their reputation as fighting men remained fully "secured."

CHAPTER **13**

THE ENEMY

The Soviet-directed Oriental taught us a great deal about himself in the period between June and December of 1950. He did this through a series of stinging defeats. It is true that in many battles he outnumbered us overwhelmingly. But the enemy's strength is not in numbers alone.

In Korea the oriental peasant, both Chinese and Korean, showed that he could drive a tank, lob a mortar, and fire a machine gun with deadly efficiency. I remember talking to a marine in the Naktong River bulge who said ruefully, "Those gooks can land a mortar right in your hip pocket."

In addition, the enemy can fight on about one fifth of what the United States Army presently considers necessary. The enemy's army has a minimum number of housekeeping and supply services. Beer and mail are not received in front-line foxholes. Trucks carrying goodies from the Post Exchange do not clog the enemy's roads. The proportion of administrative officers to combat officers is low. More soldiers are required to shoot and fewer to do paper work than in the American Army. By our standards, the enemy's medical corps is primitive. But he is accustomed to privation and dirt and has great powers of endurance. The slogan of the Chinese soldier is typical: "First we suffer, then we enjoy."

Probably the greatest achievement of the Chinese and North Korean dictatorship is the quality of their officers. Here their system of intensive political indoctrination has certainly paid off. The fanaticism of the officers often kept the North Koreans and Chinese fighting under circumstances in which the enlisted men were eager to surrender.

There was little fundamental difference between the North Korean soldier and the Chinese soldier. This is not surprising, since the nucleus of the North Korean Army was trained in the Chinese Eighth Route Army. If anything, the Chinese were a little smarter, a little better disciplined than the Koreans.

The enemy made maximum use of his great manpower advantage for the infiltration and encirclement of our forces. They combined guerilla tactics with a shrewd use of modern weapons. They used psychological warfare to advantage. They made the most of night attacks, in which assaults were launched to the blowing of bugles, and squads controlled by the shriek of whistles. An amazing number of Chinese and Koreans spoke a little English. These men would strip overcoats and parkas from our dead soldiers and try to make us believe they were friends. Others learned to yell "medic, medic" and trick us into revealing our positions.

Private Carrol Brewer told me of one tactic used by the Chinese in the marine battle out of Yudamni. "They would let us into their foxholes and disappear over a hill. Then at night they would come back by the thousands. And they'd wait until they were practically on top of you before they'd shoot."

They frequently seemed to care very little for life and were willing to die unquestioningly. They would keep right on surging toward a target even though wave after wave of them were blown up in the process.

In their encircling and nipping-off tactics, the Communists often won rich prizes in American equipment. When the enemy broke through our lines on the Kum River, for instance, they scooped up ammunition, artillery guns, machine guns, recoilless weapons, and mortars. The Chinese winter break-through also gave them substantial booty.

This capture of our weapons enabled the enemy to hold out at the beginning in spite of our heavy bombing of North Korean bases. The Communists didn't have to depend on supplies from home bases. They were getting them from us.

The Chinese, and particularly the North Koreans, forage much of what they need in the way of food and services as they go along. They make the local population carry ammunition and cook their food. (It was only very late in the summer that Americans learned to use local citizenry for ammo bearers.) They make use of every conceivable beast of burden, even camels.

The complaint against the Russians made by the German General von Manteuffel could well be repeated against the Reds in Korea. Von Manteuffel said of the Russian Army: "You can't stop them, like an ordinary army, by cutting their communications, because you so rarely find any supply columns to cut."

By comparison with the enemy, the American Army is road-bound. General Dean of the 24th Division put the problem very neatly when he said, "How am I going to teach these boys that they can't all jeep to battle?"

The Chinese were very short of heavy equipment in the first phases of their intervention. They had to rely mainly on machine guns and grenades, although they did turn American light bazookas against us very effectively. If the numerical odds had been anywhere near even, their lack of heavy equipment could have been a handicap to them. But as it was, their shortage of heavy artillery made it possible for them to hike at night over mountain trails, with the guns and packs on their backs. Then, with the enormous advantage of surprise, they could jump our troops at will.

Five years of political indoctrination had put highly effective intellectual blinders on North Korean officers. I was impressed by a talk I had with one North Korean

lieutenant. He was among a group of wounded prisoners
of war whom I interviewed in our base hospital at Pusan.

"The only reason I am here is because I was uncon-
scious when I was captured," he said. "I would never have
surrendered of my own will. I believed with all my heart
that I was doing the right thing by fighting for the unifi-
cation of my country. I believed the people in South Korea were oppressed."

The lieutenant himself was ragged and covered with
sores, and he now indicated to the interpreter, an American missionary, that he wanted to say more. It may have
been for my benefit, but he added, "Now that I've talked
to South Koreans, I believe that all the things we were
taught are not true. I feel pity for those who are still fighting, because they do not know the truth."

Apparently this indoctrination is not completely shared,
as yet, by the rank and file. Many North Korean enlisted
men surrendered. The marines, completely surrounded
by the enemy at Hagaru, had a pleasant surprise when
two hundred Chinese came voluntarily into camp.

These POWs were reassuring evidence that the enemy
was only human. When I was at Koto there were nearly
three hundred Chinese POWs in the improvised stockade.
I wanted to find out why they seemed to survive the
frightful cold better than we did. The answer was that
they didn't. Their feet were black with frostbite, and the
gangrenous odor of rotting flesh filled the stockade air.

While I was in the stockade a wounded Chinese was
brought in on a stretcher. His arms were bent at the el-

bow, and his hands and feet were frozen marble solid. He was groaning rhythmically.

A wizened Chinese corporal plucked at my sleeve and pointed to his moaning countryman. "That is why we surrender," he said.

These Chinese captured on the northeast front generally wore only tennis shoes and several pairs of socks. Naturally their feet suffered, but the rest of their uniforms —quilted jackets and pants—seemed to keep them sufficiently warm.

The Chinese who surrendered to us in the northeast were the weakest link in the Communist enemy command. Significantly, none ranked higher than corporal. They all said that they had been forced to fight. But this claim may be more representative of innate Chinese diplomacy than the truth. I asked, through my interpreter, Lieutenant Paul Y. Kim, if any of them wanted to go back to China.

All the prisoners gestured "No." The corporal, the oldest of the group and its spokesman, recited reasons that have become decidedly familiar. "We were poor under Chiang," he said, "but now we are both poor and cannot do as we want. We cannot move freely from village to village. Many are arrested. We do not wish to fight for the Communists."

These Chinese POWs were ignorant men but they had a very clear idea of their country's relationship to Russia.

"The Russians," said the old corporal, with a distressed

sweep of his hands, "are everywhere in China, but especially at the airfields. And it is they who decide."

The original North Korean Army that struck southward on June twenty-fifth probably totaled close to one hundred and fifty thousand men. Even without air power and without sea power, they mauled us badly until the Inchon landing.

Then the Chinese armies stepped in. The Chinese Peoples Liberation Army consists of five million men. But Far Eastern experts say that only two million of these are first-rate front-line troops. These are organized in a system of five field armies.

The Fourth Field Army, the first to intervene in Korea, is led by General Lin Piao. He is forty-two years old and graduated from the Whampoa Military Academy at Canton. He began fighting for the Communists in 1927 and is considered one of Peking's best commanders. The Third Field Army, also in Korea, is led by General Chen Yi, who previously held command of East China.

These forces are not only the best trained but also the best equipped in China. Much of their equipment is American. They seized many American bazookas, jeeps, trucks, and fieldpieces in Manchuria and they captured many American weapons from the Chinese Nationalists. They also took over Japanese supplies left behind in Manchuria. The Russians have provided them with tanks. And the Chinese air force, which probably totaled only five hundred planes in January of 1951, may soon be rapidly expanded.

We relearned from the Chinese what we had discovered in fighting the North Koreans. Air power and artillery are not enough when you are vastly outnumbered in mountainous terrain. Even the marines, fully supported by air and equipped with the best American weapons, could not cope with the masses of howling, bugle-blowing Chinese. In the mountains of East Korea ill-equipped Chinese pushed the marines back by sheer weight of numbers. Marine close-support planes, striking sometimes within thirty-five feet of the front lines, saved thousands of lives and won many skirmishes. But the planes could not win the day.

One of the "Eight Rules of Conduct" laid down by Peking provides for the good treatment of captives. It is the Communist theory that this contributes to victory. From time to time the Chinese have made token releases of prisoners, in the hope that the prisoners would report their good treatment and encourage our soldiers to give up. The Chinese were certainly far more correct in their behavior toward captives than were the North Koreans. This is not surprising, as both North and South Koreans are notorious for their cruelty.

I do not believe that the Chinese treatment of prisoners reflects any innate softheartedness. It is a tactic. When barbarism served the purpose better, the Chinese did not hesitate. They certainly caused inhuman suffering by their practice of hurling hand grenades into ambulances, and on one occasion they set fire to a gasoline-soaked truckload of American wounded.

The North Koreans gave the local population the full Communist treatment. Their police-state techniques were far more ruthless than those I had seen in Poland. The Reds seemed in a greater hurry in Korea—perhaps they reasoned that the people had had such a short experience with individual freedom that a return to despotism would not meet with much resistance.

In Seoul the North Koreans jailed key clergymen, including Bishop Patrick J. Byrne. One Catholic priest was murdered and most of the rest were deported to the North. One explanation for this bold persecution is undoubtedly that the Christians are only about a million strong, a decided minority. The Reds must have felt in a position to make an all-out attack against the Church without arousing too much popular indignation.

The Reds were also astute at using food as a political weapon. They took over all stocks of rice. Then families whose children joined the Communist League got special ration cards. The same was true of workers who enrolled in Communist unions.

The invaders carried on a systematic terror campaign against all people who had ever been associated with Americans. Many thousand alleged "pro-Americans" were thrown into prison and all their property was confiscated. The Seoul newspapers were labeled pro-American and their plants annexed by the Reds.

Their formula for taking over the government of the important cities was the same everywhere. A municipal administration, complete with mayor and cabinet, was formed in Pyongyang and sent to the city immediately after capture. All key posts were filled by trusted emissaries from the North. Sometimes local elections were held, carefully designed to make the conquered areas an integral part of the northern government.

In some places the Reds issued decrees dispossessing landowners who held more than a certain prescribed acreage. In the short period of the first occupation they were unable to do a thorough job of this. Their decrees aroused little enthusiasm because they were coupled with very high crop-delivery requirements.

One way the Communists really made themselves unpopular was by introducing forced conscription of young men into the North Korean Army. They would go into houses and farm dwellings at night and, often at pistol point, force young Koreans to march off to training centers.

At Hagaru we had an example of local hostility toward the invading Chinese armies. Colonel Bankson Holcomb, 1st Marine Division intelligence officer, told me that some of the townspeople had actually come to him and asked him to burn their homes so that the Chinese could not get them. Of course he didn't do it, but it was an interesting insight into the depth of their feeling.

The pitiful swarms of refugees who fled South in the wake of our retreating army were irrefutable evidence of how much the people feared the Reds. They waded across icy streams and crawled painfully across broken ridges rather than stay at home and face the Communists. At the Hungan beachhead Rear Admiral Doyle radioed to Tokyo, "My personal observation is that if the lift were available we could denude North Korea of its civilian population. Almost all of them want to go to South Korea."

In my first visit to Seoul in May of 1950 there were a number of Korean newspapermen who believed some of the Communist propaganda. They felt that unity was better than two antagonistic Koreas, even if it meant Communist domination. I tried to revisit some of these men when the second Red siege of Seoul was threatening. But their taste of Red rule between June and September had been enough. They had been among the first to go south, and I could not find them.

It is true, of course, that in the early days of the Chinese Communist struggle the agrarian reforms won much popular support in China. Probably the Chinese must have been comparatively gentle in their demands for compulsory crop deliveries. They were seeking to win over the Chinese people by persuasion. But the Reds in Korea were backed from the start by the Soviet. They had absolute power and did not need to persuade. In any event, the Korean farmers with whom I talked near Wŏnsan and in the Hungnam Hamhung Plain expressed great bitterness against the government. They claimed that taxes and quotas were so, high that there was nothing left for their own families. After our December retreat from the North thousands of farmers abandoned their own land to become propertyless refugees in South Korea.

It is high time to evaluate what these months in Korea

have taught us. Korea has proved decisively to the world that the oriental peasant is an efficient fighting man and that the new militarism of China has produced a first-class army.

Until now the democratic world has relied on technological supremacy and the possession of superior firearms to win its battles with the oriental world. Now the oriental world has most of these weapons, in addition to man power. The Chinese are a powerful instrument of the Soviet, which has boldly attacked the United States and the United Nations.

By challenging us with force, the enemy has confronted the free world with a series of choices, all of them unpleasant.

CHAPTER **14**

THE PROSPECT IS WAR

If we cede the Asian mainland to the Communists without a fight, we will greatly strengthen our enemy. We will
give the Chinese military dictatorship time to build an
even stronger and better army. We will give them the opportunity to "liberate" the rich prizes of Indo-China and
Thailand. But we will not be giving them only man
power and raw materials. We will be giving them something of great strategic importance. If we pull out of
Asia, we say to the Soviet world, "Your eastern flank is
now comparatively secure. Go ahead and concentrate on
Europe."

If we do the Soviet world this favor, Europe will eventually go under. And when that happens, if America con-
tinues to sit back, naïvely waiting for the Soviet dictatorships to crack from within, it is only a matter of time

before the entire world will become a string of Soviet socialist dictatorships.

All of this might take from twenty to fifty years. But it would happen eventually because of an old-fashioned precept known as the balance of power. The Soviets would have so many more people and resources than we would that they could attack us and win. It's one world, all right, but not the way Wendell Willkie meant. It's either our world or their world. The Soviet powers have shown us that this particular planet has become too small to exist half slave, half free.

I have watched seven modern police states at work, and I cannot place any hope on an internal crack-up in the dictatorships. A modern dictatorship has a monopoly of mass communications and almost complete control over men's minds. Hitler's Reich was crushed only by defeat on the battlefield. Resistance movements do not spring up until there is hope of liberation. Europe lay submissively in Hitler's grasp until the American invasion of North Africa.

In ancient times, when dictators were separated from their subordinates by days of travel, they had to allow their underlings some individual initiative. In that small freedom lay the possibilities for revolt. But today Moscow controls east Berlin by long-distance telephone. The slightest deviation from the rules will be reported immediately, and punishment can be dealt out with equal swiftness.

The alternative to appeasement in Asia is to fight a series of holding actions. At the same time we must work at top speed to rectify our critical lack of trained man power and our lack of weapons. By continuing to harass the enemy in the Far East we will keep alive the hope of anti-Communist countries.

If we build up our strength quickly enough, perhaps the inevitable showdown can be diplomatic. But we must prepare for the worst.

Our preparations must be political as well as military. We must help other nations to help themselves, so that the non-Communist way of life is something worth fighting for. We must turn our back on colonialism everywhere and, in this common struggle against the dictatorships, we must give every partner honorable status. This is particularly important in the Far East, where we are faced with a surging nationalistic spirit on which the Reds have capitalized. There is no need for the Communists to capture these countries in revolt against old imperialisms. America should put herself squarely on the side of those nations asking national independence and self-government, and do all she can to help them economically.

Politically speaking, time is beginning to be on our side. The Communists in Asia have begun to discredit themselves. It is not lost on the average Chinese, for example, that his great new "liberation" has been capped by the greatest inflow of Russians in important posts that China has ever seen. Oppressed people who apathetically assumed that Communists couldn't be worse than what they had before are rapidly beginning to regard the Reds as the greater of two evils.

You can't have a working democracy where people are starving. Hunger breeds desperation; desperation breeds violence; violence breeds a police state.

And let no American feel that anything he does for the rest of the world is charity. We urgently need as many people as possible on our side. Since we are not a dictatorship and have to persuade rather than browbeat, America must prove by concrete acts that the people of the world have more to gain by siding with her than with the new militaristic dictatorships of the Soviet Union and its satellites.

The Korean war taught us another very important lesson: we can no longer substitute machines for men. It is a grave worry to many officers at the fighting front that the people back home haven't grasped this fact. Men like Colonel Michaelis, Colonel Stephens, and General Church believe that if we make use of what we have learned in Korea we can fight many successful holding actions. But the endurance and will of the individual are all-important.

A German general, talking about the French failure in 1870, described exactly what we must avoid. "The people had always concentrated on matériel questions," he said. "They thought that the offensive power of the enemy would be broken by the defensive action of new and terrible weapons. In that way they ruined the spirit of their army."

The main thing America should mass-produce is courage. We need the kind of spirit that made Marine Sergeant Robert Ward ask his mother to let him leave his safe desk job and go back to his platoon.

"I'm no hero," Sergeant Ward wrote, "but if these people aren't stopped here on their own ground, we will have to share the thing which so many have died to prevent their loved ones from sharing—the sight of death in our own back yards, of women and children being victims of these people. I went on the warpath for the right to do my bit to keep our people free and proud, and now I'm shackled to a useless job. I ask you, my mother, to free me so I can once again be free to help my boys. They placed their faith in me . . . and whenever I led them I brought them all back. Now someone else leads them and I know they need me. Maybe in a sense I need them—my dirty, stinking, and loyal platoon."

Many more Americans will have to be tough enough and spirited enough to want to fight these dirty, stinking battles. We are engaged in a kind of international endurance contest, and the Communists are the first to recognize it. They believe that the comforts of our capitalist way of life have so softened us that our lack of self-discipline will help to defeat us. A North Korean colonel, who had spent some time in the United States, expressed this widespread belief in our decadence very well when he told me, "Your countrymen will be defeated by a longing for a hot shower."

In his book, *Strategic Problems of China's Revolutionary War,* Mao Tse-tung stated his contempt for the staying power of non-Communist armies. He wrote, "The theory that the massing of a great army is limited by terrain, roads, supplies and by billeting facilities should be taken with great discretion. These limitations have a different application in the Red army than in the non-Communist army. For the Red army can undergo greater hardship than the latter."

Then he added a remark which we would do well to remember: "A Soviet war lasting ten years may be surprising to other countries, but to us this is only the preface."

Certainly Americans are comfort-loving. And perhaps too many soldiers have been coddled into believing that USO shows are essential to their fighting ability. But the marines at Hagaru, and countless other individual American regiments, have shown the ferocity with which our soldiers can fight when they are well trained, have confidence in their leaders, and have learned to face the brutal fact that many must accept death.

In a conversation recorded by Harold Martin of the *Saturday Evening Post,* Colonel Michaelis summarized what was wrong with the American soldier in Korea.

"When I took command of my regiment at Pusan, I found myself in a pretty depressing assignment," Michaelis said. "I was new. My executive officer was new. Some of the officers—only a few—were seeing green grasshoppers on their shoulders at the very thought of going to war. These had to be weeded out and sent back to desk jobs.

"The troops were green. Most of them had only eight months' service behind them. They came in with their duffel bags loaded down. The officers carried foot lockers. As a paratrooper I had learned that you have to travel and fight lightly loaded if you are going to fight at all. We had to have a general shakedown. We had all kinds of special gear—violins, banjos, God knows what all. There must have been eight carloads of junk shaken out of the regiment before we started north. But when we started out we traveled like a fighting soldier ought to travel. Each man had his weapon, his ammunition, his blanket, shelter half, mess gear, razor, soap, and towels, and an extra pair of socks. That was all and that was enough.

"In peacetime training we've gone in for too much damn falderal. We've put too much stress on information and education and not enough stress on rifle marksmanship and scouting and patrolling and the organization of a defense position. These kids of mine have all the guts in the world and I can count on them to fight. But when they started out they couldn't shoot. They didn't know their weapons. They have not had enough training in plain, old-fashioned musketry. They'd spent a lot of time listening to lectures on the difference between Communism and Americanism and not enough time crawling on their bellies on maneuvers with live ammunition singing over them. They'd been nursed and coddled, told to drive safely, to buy War Bonds, to avoid VD, to write a letter home to mother, when somebody ought to have been telling them how to clear a machine gun when it jams. They've had to learn in combat, in a matter of days, the basic things they should have known before they ever faced an enemy. And some of them don't learn fast enough."

The demoralization that sometimes gripped these green troops seems to be the direct result of too much coddling and not enough tough training. Toughness on the battle-field is important because it saves lives. There will have to be equal toughness at home.

We shall have to face the prospect of a decade of wars. It helps to remember that, for Mao Tse-tung, a ten-year war is only the preface. And we will have to face the prospect of a decade of austerity. In this era it is no longer a question of how much our economy can stand but how much is needed to survive.

We will certainly produce anything that is needed. I refuse to accept the idea that Americans are so decadent that they prefer a way of life that will give them a new automobile each year rather than a way of life that will protect them from the midnight knock of the secret po-liceman, from the concentration camp, from slave-labor camps.

The word "alarmist" has come into disrepute in America. Perhaps this is because we like what we've got, and don't want to believe that we should be alarmed. I think the word should come back into good standing: we need more alarmists. My great worry is that the alarm will not be sounded in time. It seems to me that our leaders should have started preparing us for possible war the mo-ment that Russia slammed down the blockade in Berlin in 1948. Russia showed then that she was prepared to use force. It is a mockery for Truman to tell the nation that three and a half million soldiers can protect us when every responsible officer knows that it will be closer to fourteen million if we want to win.

Like any American, I realize that the strain of preparing for total war is a threat to freedom. But it is a threat which I think we can handle. Our habits of free speech and a free press are deep enough to permit us to marshal our forces against the Soviet world without ourselves becoming a dictatorship.

Until now, the two great oceans have protected Americans from the danger that war could land in their own back yards. Now there is no safe place in the world. In a matter of minutes New York could become a more ghastly deathtrap than a front-line regimental command post.

The war in Korea has made it clear that the Communists will resort to force of arms whenever and wherever they think the non-Communist world is an easy mark. Now we must mobilize so that we can stop them with our superior strength. In Korea we have paid a high price for unpreparedness. Victory will cost a lot too. But it will be cheaper than defeat.

Printed in the USA
CPSIA information can be obtained
at www.ICGtesting.com
LVHW041738280124
769859LV00015B/177